HOCKEY TRIVIA

DON WEEKES

GREY**S**TONE BOOKS

Douglas & McIntyre

Vancouver/Toronto

For Karen, Doug and baby Michael

Greystone Books
A division of Douglas & McIntyre Ltd.
1615 Venables Street
Vancouver, British Columbia V5L 2H1

The publisher gratefully acknowledges the assistance of the Canada Council and the British Columbia Ministry of Tourism, Small Business and Culture for its publishing programs.

Canadian Cataloguing in Publication Data

Weekes, Don
  Hockey trivia

"Greystone Books."
ISBN 1-55054-146-3
 1. National Hockey League—Miscellanea. 2. Miscellanea. I. Title
GV847.W43 1994   796.962   C94-910465-5

Editing by Brian Scrivener
Design by Eric Ansley & Associates Ltd.
Typesetting by Fiona MacGregor
Cover photo by Scott Levy/Bruce Bennett Studios
Printed and bound in Canada by Best Book Manufacturers, Inc.
Printed on acid-free paper

Don Weekes *is a Montreal television producer/writer with* CFCF-TV *12's nationally syndicated sports magazine, "Hockey World."*

CONTENTS

PREFACE

In October 1993, a record crowd of 27,227 show up at the ThunderDome in St. Petersburg to watch the Florida Panthers and the Tampa Bay Lightning play the first-ever Battle of Florida. In March 1994, Russian goalie Andrei Trefilov and Latvian-born Arturs Irbe start against each other in nets in an NHL game in Calgary. Six of 1993's top ten picks ink rookie contracts worth a combined $30 million.

Welcome to the new NHL. Where Russia's superstar, Sergei Fedorov, copped the league's MVP honour. Where 16% of hockey fans in South Florida are Hispanic. And where teams like San Jose have initiated street hockey programs that attract tens of thousands of kids interested in the game's basics.

As NHL commissioner Gary Bettman likes to say: Hockey is no longer the cold-weather sport. It has come in from the frozen backyard rinks of the Canadian shield to warm the hearts and stoke the competitive nature of a new American fan-base, at the grass-roots level (with rollerblade parks) and in the big leagues. Not only has the NHL gone SRO, but minor pro leagues are enjoying a renaissance, targeting markets from Birmingham to Tacoma and averaging respectable attendances with hard-hitting hockey at family prices. Moreover, franchises that once sold for $50,000 in the International Hockey League now go for a cool $6 million.

Not surprisingly, hockey's fast-paced game has already been wired for the next video generation. Sophisticated animations bring arena action to vivid life in video games with gameplay elements that use artificial intelligence to make the computer-controlled goalies harder to beat.

A message for hockey purists who shake their heads in disbelief: chill out. The game, with or without shootouts, will *never* be what it once was. And that's okay for the real fans, as long as we don't forget who and what made the game great—and what makes it greater. Times change: Gretzky is the new all-time scoring leader and the Rangers have won their long-overdue Cup. What could possibly happen next? A weighted lottery draft? Yes, it's coming.

The game is evolving, and *Hockey Trivia* has come up with the most current and offbeat trivia questions imaginable, working in brand-new statistical data and oddball anecdotes while presenting hard-core facts and records that have become standard in the game.

In *Hockey Trivia*, we ask the most up-to-date questions about your favourite players and teams; and we toss a couple of zingers your way to see how well you remember famous hockey events from yesteryear. The best part is that, even if you don't know the answer, there's a good chance to be right with multiple choice.

And now, we would like to have your hockey questions and comments. Send along your favourite trivia question by filling out the mail-in form at the back of the book. Your question may be in next year's edition!

Many years ago, when one-time NHL president Red Dutton was still playing his rugged brand of hockey with the Maroons, his impatience over a delayed game start got the better of him. He yelled at the referee, who was hunting for game pucks: "Never mind the god-damned puck, let's start the game!"

Enough said. Let the games begin . . .

DON WEEKES
July 1994

1

THE PRE-SEASON TRYOUTS

In this warm-up quiz, we work on your conditioning and check your heart rate after a sprint around the rink on a variety of trivia topics: from scoring and goaltending statistics to hockey fact and fiction about coaches, European players and big time fights. Remember: don't expect to know all the answers, the trick is to pick the multiple choice statement that best fits.

(Answers are on page 7)

1.1 **On average, how many faceoffs are there in an NHL game?**
A. 60 to 70
B. 70 to 80
C. 80 to 90
D. 90 to 100

1.2 **What NHL venue offers the least expensive ticket prices?**
A. San Jose Arena
B. Winnipeg Arena
C. New Jersey's Meadowlands Arena
D. Tampa Bay's ThunderDome

1.3 **How many players, if any, have scored their first NHL goal on a penalty shot?**
A. Only one
B. Three
C. Five
D. It has never happened.

1.4   **Who was the first European-trained player to be named an NHL team captain?**
A. The Jets' Thomas Steen
B. The Nordiques' Peter Stastny
C. The Jets' Lars-Eric Sjoberg
D. The Atlanta Flames' Kent Nilsson

1.5   **In 1,092 NHL games in 1993–94, how many fights were called?**
A. Between 500 and 600 fights
B. Between 600 and 700 fights
C. Between 700 and 800 fights
D. More than 800 fights

1.6   **Which coach was known as "Captain Video?"**
A. Roger Neilson
B. Scotty Bowman
C. Glen Sather
D. Al Arbour

1.7   **How loud can fans get at hockey games?**
A. 100 decibels—equal to standing next to a busy expressway.
B. 112 decibels—equal to a jet taking off
C. 117 decibels—equal to a roll of thunder
D. 120 decibels—equal to a heavy metal rock concert

1.8   **Which player scored the most goals for an expansion team in its first NHL season?**
A. Hartford's Blaine Stoughton in 1979–80
B. Florida's Bob Kudelski in 1993–94
C. Tampa Bay's Brian Bradley in 1992–93
D. Edmonton's Wayne Gretzky in 1979–80

1.9 What was the age of the youngest head coach in NHL history? (Hint: it happened in 1979.)
   A. Under 30 years old
   B. 32 years old
   C. 34 years old
   D. 36 years old

1.10 Which two brothers combined to appear in the most NHL games?
   A. Phil and Tony Esposito
   B. Marty and Matt Pavelich
   C. Maurice and Henri Richard
   D. Frank and Pete Mahovlich

1.11 Who is Hobey Baker?
   A. Hockey's most traded American player
   B. Hockey's first American superstar
   C. Hockey's first American-born player to play in the Soviet Elite League
   D. The first American to win the NHL's scoring race

1.12 Which Hall-of-Famer has the most penalty minutes?
   A. Gordie Howe
   B. Eddie Shore
   C. Sprague Cleghorn
   D. Ted Lindsay

1.13 Steve Larmer was how many games short of breaking Doug Jarvis's ironman mark (964 consecutive games) before his streak ended in 1993–94?
   A. Less than 50 games
   B. 50 to 75 games
   C. 76 to 100 games
   D. More than 100 games

1.14 **Which Soviet player was the first to have his number retired in Russia?**
A. Vladimir Krutov
B. Vladislav Tretiak
C. Anatoli Tarasov
D. Valery Kharlamov

1.15 **How many American-born players have scored five goals in a single NHL game?**
A. Only one
B. Three
C. Five
D. Seven

1.16 **How much money in total did rookies of the Montreal Canadiens have to shell out at a team dinner in 1994?**
A. $2,000
B. $4,000
C. $6,000
D. $8,000

1.17 **How long (in minutes/seconds) did the Bob Probert-Marty McSorley duke-'em-out fight fest last on February 4, 1994?**
A. 0:40
B. 1:00
C. 1:40
D. 2:00

1.18 **Why were Penguins' Syl Apps Jr., Lowell MacDonald, and Jean Pronovost called the "Century Line" in the 1970s?**
A. Their line scored 100 goals plus in 1973–74.
B. Their ages totalled 100 years.
C. Each scored his 100th NHL goal in 1974–75 .
D. Their jersey numbers added up to 100.

1.19 Who is New Jersey goalie Martin Brodeur's father?
A. The Senators' goaltending coach
B. The Devils' team physiologist/conditioning coach
C. The Canadiens' team photographer
D. The NHL's European director for Central Scouting

1.20 Which former NHL star is the commissioner of Roller Hockey International?
A. Ralph Backstrom
B. Tiger Williams
C. Garry Unger
D. Bernie Federko

1.21 What was Boston's "Kraut Line" renamed during World War Two?
A. The Kitchener Kids
B. The K Line
C. The Ontario Power Line
D. The Sauerkraut Line

1.22 How many, if any, North American NHL regulars wore jersey No. 13 in 1993–94?
A. None
B. Only one
C. Three
D. Five

1.23 Which Canadian singer wrote these song lyrics:
"When he was a kid, he'd be up at five
Take shots till eight, make the thing drive
Out after school, back on ice
That was his life,
He was gonna play in the Big League."
A. k.d. Lang
B. Stompin' Tom Connors
C. Tom Cochrane
D. Bryan Adams

1.24 How many former WHA players were still playing in the NHL in 1993–94? (The WHA folded in 1979.)
A. Only one
B. Five
C. Seven
D. Ten

1.25 Which coach formed Detroit's Production Line?
A. Jimmy Skinner
B. Jack Adams
C. Sid Abel
D. Tommy Ivan

1.26 Who scored the final goal in Chicago Stadium history?
A. Tony Amonte
B. Mike Gartner
C. Steve Yzerman
D. Ray Bourque

THE PRE-SEASON TRYOUTS
Answers

1.1 B. 70 to 80.
A typical game today averages just over 70 faceoffs, a considerable increase since the 1950s, when dropping the puck to start or resume play occurred around 60 times per match. The rise in faceoffs is due to more shots on net, an increase in number of goals scored and a greater frequency in play stoppage along the boards and in the corners.

1.2 D. Tampa Bay's ThunderDome.
When the expansion Marlins of Major League Baseball went to Miami instead of Tampa Bay, it left Tampa/St. Petersburg with a $139-million teflon-domed stadium and no professional sports franchise—until the Lightning struck a deal to temporarily move into the 28,000-seat facility. Tickets in the upper deck sold for $8 to $10 and as an added bonus the Lightning sold 2,000 season tickets for $99 each, or $2.75 per home game. They are the cheapest seats in the NHL—and the farthest away from the ice.

1.3 B. Three.
Since the rule was instituted in 1934, only three NHLers have ever scored their first goals on penalty shots.

FIRST NHL GOALS ON PENALTY SHOTS			
Year	Player	Team	Goalie Beaten
1934	Ralph Bowman	St. Louis	Alex Connell
1981	Ilkka Sinisalo	Flyers	Paul Harrison
1992	Reggie Savage	Capitals	Jon Casey

1.4 **C. The Jets' Lars-Eric Sjoberg.**
When the NHL and WHA merged in 1979, Swedish-born Sjoberg extended his four-year tenure as captain of the WHA Jets to become the first European-trained player to wear the "C" on an NHL team, the 1979–80 Winnipeg Jets. A veteran of Sweden's elite league when he joined the WHA Jets in 1974–75, Sjoberg, 30, ascended to the captaincy the following year and remained Winnipeg's leader until retiring in 1980. Stastny and Steen are the second and third Europeans to captain NHL teams. Nilsson played as a Flame, both in Atlanta and Calgary, but was never captain.

1.5 **D. More than 800 fights.**
There were about 821 scraps in 1993–94, resulting in 1,643 majors for an average of 1.50 fighting majors per game (FPG), an increase over 1992–93 (1.25 FPG) but down from 1984–85 (1.87 FPG). Instigators were identified 104 times or about 13% of all fights. As in previous years, fisticuffs decreased as the season progressed and were limited during the playoffs.

1.6 **A. Roger Neilson.**
Neilson began hiring college kids to shoot game film while coaching the Peterborough Petes of the OHA in the late 1960s and continued the practice in the NHL where he became one of the first coaches to use video-tape to analyze team performance, earning him the nickname "Captain Video." Soon more NHL teams hired cameramen and adopted video as a source to study playmaking, until the 1980s when the league made it obligatory for all clubs to provide game tapes.

1.7 **C. 117 decibels— equal to a roll of thunder.**
During the 5–2 playoff win over the Maple Leafs at San Jose Arena in May 1994, the Sharks' decibel meter verified the fan noise level at 117 db—equal to a roll of thunder. Perhaps the loudest hockey facility was the

old Chicago Stadium. Its Barton Organ (the pipes of which were built into the Stadium's rafters) when cranked up, could reach 130 db, or sound you could actually feel.

1.8 A. Hartford's Blaine Stoughton in 1979–80.
Stoughton scored 56 goals in the Whalers' inaugural NHL season, tying Buffalo's Danny Gare and Los Angeles' Charlie Simmer for the 1979–80 lead. Stoughton also became the first 50-goal man with an expansion club on March 28, 1980, outpacing Gretzky, who scored goal No. 50 just five days later. Gretzky totalled 51 goals that year, Bradley potted 42 goals in 1992–93, while Kudelski hit the 40-goal mark in 1993–94.

1.9 A. Under 30 years old.
When the Washington Capitals hired Gary Green in November 1979, he was 26 years old, the youngest NHL bench boss ever. Green, already a Memorial Cup-winning coach with the Peterborough Petes, had only been coaching the Caps' farm team in Hershey for a month when he got the call from the big club. Green coached 2½ seasons in Washington, finishing just out of playoff contention in 1980 and 1981.

1.10 B. Marty and Matt Pavelich.
Winner of four Stanley Cups with the Red Wings, Marty played in 634 regular season games from 1947 through 1957, while younger brother Matt officiated in 1,727 NHL games during a 23-year span (1956 to 1979). Combined the Pavelich boys (separated by six years) from Sault St. Marie appeared in 2,361 NHL games, meeting as player and on-ice official only seven times, including two playoff games, during the year their careers overlapped, 1956–57. Matt became the first linesman inducted into the Hall of Fame. Gordie Howe named his eldest son, Marty, after Pavelich, who played

on Detroit's checking line with Tony Leswick (Lenny Dykstra's uncle) and Glen Skov, brother of Art Skov, another long-time NHL official. The Richards appeared in 2,234 matches, the Espositos, 2,168 matches and the Mahovlichs, 2,065 games.

1.11 B. Hockey's first American superstar.

Hobart "Hobey" Baker was the perfect All-American collegiate sports hero. The award named after him, which goes to the U.S. college hockey player of the year, honours that individual who exhibits hockey skills on and off the ice and excels in scholastic achievement and sportsmanship, much like Hobey himself in his Princeton days. An exceptional skater and stickhandler, it was once reported that Baker, after being checked over the boards, dashed along the bench, leapt back into the action, got the loose puck and scored. Baker captained his team to two intercollegiate titles in the 1910s, but he never made the NHL. He died flying with the famous Escadrille Lafayette in World War One. Winners of the Hobey Baker Award include Neal Broten (1981), Tom Kurvers (1984) and Paul Kariya (1993).

1.12 D. Ted Lindsay.

A member of Detroit's famed Production Line (with Gordie Howe and Sid Abel), Lindsay played a major role as the Wings' physical and emotional leader, helping win seven consecutive league titles and four Stanley Cups, between 1948 and 1955. He won the Art Ross Trophy as the NHL's leading scorer in 1950, captained the Wings (1952–56), made nine all-star appearances and served more time in the penalty box than any other player in the history of the game to that date. A fearless competitor and master defense specialist, Lindsay amassed 1,808 penalty minutes over 17 seasons, more than any other Hall of Famer, including Howe (1,685 PIM), Shore (1,047 PIM) and Cleghorn (489

PIM). Lindsay was inducted into the Hall of Fame in 1966, only a year after he retired.

1.13   C. 76 to 100 games.

Larmer, with 884 consecutive games played in 11 complete seasons, was 81 games shy of breaking Jarvis's streak before a dispute with Chicago management ended his ironman run at the start of 1993–94. A player of principle, Larmer would sooner give up his hard-earned streak than settle for his new role and the new direction the club had taken under first-year head coach Darryl Sutter. Instead, he cast his fate to the trade winds, which blew him to New York and a Stanley Cup with Mike Keenan's Rangers.

1.14   B. Vladislav Tretiak.

Like much of the former Soviet Union, traditions of the Russian game are undergoing fundamental change, and a few new customs, like retiring sweater numbers, are being embraced under the influence of the North American style of play. In 1993, before a sellout crowd at Moscow's Ice Palace hockey arena, Tretiak's No. 20 was raised to the rafters in a first-ever ceremony that saw one of hockey's greatest goalies honoured for his work backstopping the Central Red Army teams of the 1970s and early 1980s.

1.15   A. Only one.

Among more than 30 players to record five-goal games in NHL history, only Mark Pavelich of Eveleth, Minnesota is U.S.-born. Pavelich's five goals were scored on a pass to the faceoff circle, a deflection, a rebound scramble, a slapshot and a riser in front of Hartford goalie Greg Millen, who played all 60 minutes and took the 11–3 loss. Pavelich's milestone, only the second in Ranger history, happened on February 23, 1983, the eve of the third anniversary of the 1980

Olympic gold-medal win by Team USA, of which Pavelich was a member.

1.16 D. $8,000.

The time-honoured tradition of hazing rookies is over, recently replaced with an idea thought up by millionaire hockey players, who've found a much more appropriate means of extracting pleasure from the new kids on the team: The Rookie Dinner. That's where the entire team goes out to a restaurant of choice for a evening of food and drink and the rookies get stiffed with the tab. At a Tampa steakhouse, Canadien rookies Pierre Sevigny, Peter Popovic, Les Kuntar and Oleg Petrov each paid $1,980 (U.S.) on a near $8,000 dinner bill. While in many respects the rookie dinner is a more sane approach to team initiation, it sometimes offers no more dignity than hazing. Especially in Kuntar's case. The rookie goalie was returned to the Canadiens' farm team in Fredericton a few days after the big night out.

1.17 C. 1:40.

Boxing aficionados say, as hockey fights go, it ranked with the "Thrilla in Manilla" and the "Rumble in the Jungle." It was a heavyweight classic: McSorley 6'-1", 235 lbs. bare-fisted it with Probert, 6'-3", 225 lbs., going toe-to-toe, launching rapid-fire blows for 1:40 until the pummelling bloodied their knuckles and complete exhaustion set in. Only after a gash opened over McSorley's right eye did the linesmen step in. Each got five minutes, and they weren't worth skatelaces for the rest of the game.

1.18 A. Their line scored 100 goals plus in 1973–74.

Often forgotten and never as flashy as Buffalo's French Connection or the Flyers' Bobby Clarke line, Pittsburgh's Century Line of Apps, Pronovost and MacDonald were among the best playmaking trios of the mid-1970s, notching 107 goals in 1973–74, second only to Phil Esposito's line in Boston.

1.19 C. The Canadiens' team photographer.
Martin Brodeur's hockey bloodlines are impeccable. His father Denis, the official club photographer of the Canadiens, tended goal for the Victoriaville Tigers when Jean Beliveau was its star centre in 1949, and, later, he won a bronze medal for Canada in international hockey at the 1956 Olympics. Although father Denis never played in the six-team NHL (a league in an era without substitute goalies when only extraordinarily talented netminders made it), his 30-year career in sports photography brought him close to his on-ice passion, almost equalling his real pride and joy, his son Martin and his success between the pipes with New Jersey.

1.20 A. Ralph Backstrom.
Among the many former NHLers in management and coaching positions at RHI is Backstrom, 17-year veteran of the Canadiens, Kings and Blackhawks and now commissioner of the fledgling 24-team roller hockey league. Along with RHI president and founder Dennis Murphy, Backstrom oversees the sports-related operations of the league.

1.21 A. The Kitchener Kids.
Because of their Germanic background, the Bruins' Milt Schmidt, Woody Dumart and Bobby Bauer became known as the "Kraut Line," a nickname that, due to anti-German reaction, fell out of favour during World War Two. The Kitchener connection evolved from the trio's place of birth in Ontario, a town settled largely by German immigrants in the 1800s, which itself went through a wartime name change. Until World War One, Kitchener had been known as Berlin, Ontario.

1.22 B. Only one.

In a profession where luck and superstition plague players into tedious minutely detailed routines, the Sharks' Jamie Baker doesn't worry, at least not about the No. 13 on his back. The Ottawa-born native is the only North American regular in the NHL to sport No. 13, an unlucky number on this side of the Atlantic but popular overseas—look at Europeans bearing No. 13s like Teemu Selanne and Mats Sundin. Wearing the bad-luck number was the inspiration of an Ottawa Senator trainer who, at the 1992 training camp, suggested Baker take it because 13 was a baker's dozen.

1.23 C. Tom Cochrane.

Every parent's dream is to see his or her children succeed. In sports, the challenge begins sooner in life and fills a parent's head with what might be, as Cochrane so aptly wrote in "Big League":

"My boy's gonna play in the Big League
My boy's gonna turn some heads
My boy's gonna play in the Big League
My boy's gonna knock 'em dead."

Cochrane's inspiration came while on tour in western Canada. Before a concert he was approached by a man whose son was a big Cochrane fan and, also, a promising hockey player with an athletic scholarship. Unfortunately, before the boy could fulfil his life-long dream of playing in the big leagues, he was killed in a car accident. Grief-stricken, the father had to meet his son's musical hero. So moved by his fellow westerner's tragedy, Cochrane penned "Big League".

1.24 C. Seven.

The remaining seven NHLers who began their hockey careers in the defunct WHA are: Wayne Gretzky (Indianapolis & Edmonton/1978–79), Mark Messier (Indianapolis & Cincinnati/1978–79), Mike Gartner (Cincinnati/1978–79), Mark Howe (Houston & New England/1973–74 to 1978–79), Rob Ramage (Birmingham/1978–79), Michel Goulet (Birmingham/1978–79) and Gordie Roberts (New England 1975–76 to 1978–79).

1.25 D. Tommy Ivan.

Although Jack Adams is often credited with forming the Production Line (he did put Sid Abel and Gordie Howe together), it wasn't until Ivan took over in 1947 (his coaching debut) that Ted Lindsay was tried as a left wing linemate. It was a match made in hockey heaven. The line gelled into the league's most dominant offensive unit, with at least one member finishing first in the NHL scoring race for five successive years, and in 1949–50, the trio going 1–2–3 among all point-getters. The original Production Line played together until 1952 when Abel became player-coach with Chicago.

1.26 B. Mike Gartner.

The last goal in Chicago Stadium's illustrious 65-year history happened on April 28, 1994 when Toronto's Mike Gartner scored a power play goal against Ed Belfour to give the Maple Leafs a 1–0 win and eliminate the Hawks in the 1994 Conference quarterfinals.

GAME 1

PASSING THE PUCK FANTASTIC

In this pinwheel game each word joins in exactly the same way as a regular crossword. Starting at square No. 1 work clockwise around each of the three concentric rings, filling in the right word answer from the clues below. Each answer begins with the last letter of the previous word (i.e., the last letter of Around No. 1 is the first letter of Around No. 3). There are also 11 word answers in Towards Centre. Each is four letters long and begins at the outer ring and heads inward.

(Solutions are on page 116)

Around

1. _____ Cup
3. Above .500 _____
5. _____ Lindros
7. _____ Rockies
10. 20-year NHLer with Wings, Bruins, Leafs and Stars, Murray _____
12. _____ Neilson
14. _____ season
16. Lanny McDonald is _____
18. Team physician (nickname)
19. Russian _____
20. _____ guy
21. Heavy _____
22. Lorne Worsley
23. Part of goal net
24. Strategy or _____
25. George Armstrong's nickname
26. Play _____

27. Ted Kennedy's nickname
28. _____'_ linemates on the French Connection were Rick Martin and Gilbert Perreault.
29. The _____ the limit
30. The Silver _____
31. Goal _____
32. _____ your limits

Towards Centre

1. Price or _____
2. Outmanoeuvre
4. Regulation or _____ of the game
6. _____ the pines
8. Starting _____up
9. A Mighty _____
11. All-stars selected by _____
13. _____-winning goal
15. _____away
16. _____ to the occasion
17. Playoff _____

16

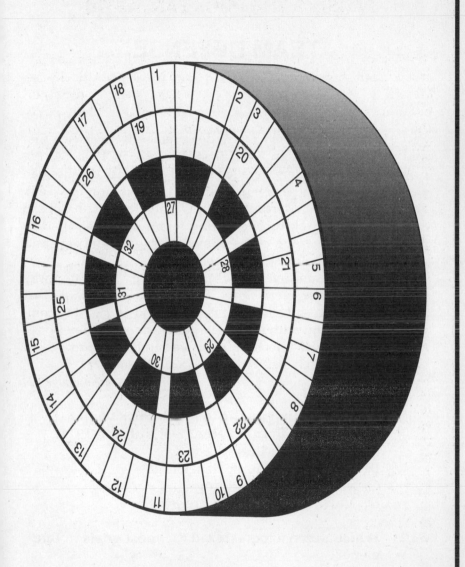

2

TEAM DEFENSE

Fact #1: At the 1994 Entry Draft, defensemen were chosen first and second overall, an NHL first. Fact #2: In 1993–94, the league's two best teams were led by and won with defensemen as top scorers, another NHL first. Fact #3: Netminders Felix Potvin, Arturs Irbe, Martin Brodeur, Patrick Roy, Kirk McLean and Dominik Hasek turned young teams into playoff contenders, gave average clubs above-average standings and made good teams almost unbeatable.

Welcome to Team Defense, where everybody plays two-way hockey to keep the game close. It's the winning formula that helped expansion clubs like the Panthers and Ducks stay competitive. On a team with minimal offense, smother the opposition, backcheck and forecheck your way into the third period when anything can happen in a low-scoring game.

(Answers are on page 22)

2.1 **Who is the first goalie to break the 2.00 GAA barrier since Bernie Parent last did it in 1974?**
  A. San Jose's Arturs Irbe
  B. Buffalo's Dominik Hasek
  C. Montreal's Patrick Roy
  D. New Jersey's Martin Brodeur

2.2 **Which defenseman scored the most goals in one game?**
  A. Ian Turnbull
  B. Bobby Orr
  C. Hap Day
  D. Paul Coffey

2.3 **Which goalie had the most shutouts in his rookie season?**
   A. George Hainsworth
   B. Tony Esposito
   C. Mike Richter
   D. Terry Sawchuk

2.4 **Since 1924, how often, if ever, has the Hart Trophy (league MVP) been awarded to a player on a last-place team?**
   A. Never
   B. Two times
   C. Four times
   D. Six times

2.5 **Which goalie set the NHL record for most shots faced in one season?**
   A. Tim Cheveldae
   B. Craig Billington
   C. Curtis Joseph
   D. Bob Essensa

2.6 **Who was the first NHL defenseman in history to lead a first place team (overall) in scoring?**
   A. The Bruins' Ray Bourque
   B. The Rangers' Sergei Zubov
   C. The Islanders' Denis Potvin
   D. The Devils' Scott Stevens

2.7 **What is the most number of losses one NHL goaltender has endured in one season?**
   A. Between 35 and 40 losses
   B. Between 40 and 45 losses
   C. Between 45 and 50 losses
   D. More than 50 losses

2.8 Who was the first NHL rearguard to score 500 points in a career?
  A. Doug Harvey
  B. Red Kelly (as a Red Wing)
  C. Bobby Orr
  D. Bill Gadsby

2.9 Which two goalies were opponents in the 1964 Stanley Cup finals, yet won the Vezina Trophy as teammates the following year?
  A. Johnny Bower & Don Simmons
  B. Jacques Plante & Glenn Hall
  C. Terry Sawchuk & Johnny Bower
  D. Roger Crozier & Terry Sawchuk

2.10 Only one NHL team from 1993–94 had all its players in the plus column. Which club?
  A. The Detroit Red Wings
  B. The New Jersey Devils
  C. The Toronto Maple Leafs
  D. The New York Rangers

2.11 In NHL history, how many defensemen have had 100-point seasons?
  A. Two
  B. Three
  C. Four
  D. Five

2.12 Which goalie has won the most NHL games?
  A. Tony Esposito
  B. Terry Sawchuk
  C. Jacques Plante
  D. Glenn Hall

2.13 Between Butch and Pierre Bouchard, how many goals did father and son score in their combined 23-year career with the Canadiens?
A. Less than 50 goals
B. 50 to 100 goals
C. 100 to 200 goals
D. More than 200 goals

2.14 Which NHL D-man held the scoring record for most points in a season before Bobby Orr broke it 1968–69?
A. Pierre Pilote
B. Babe Pratt
C. Doug Mohns
D. Red Kelly (as a Red Wing)

2.15 Which goaltender has allowed the most goals in NHL history?
A. Gilles Meloche
B. Rogatien Vachon
C. Tony Esposito
D. Greg Millen

2.16 Who was the first defenseman in playoff history to record a playoff hat trick?
A. Calgary's Paul Reinhart
B. Boston's Bobby Orr
C. Montreal's Eric Desjardins
D. The Islanders' Denis Potvin

2.17 Which NHL team first employed a defense system that forced opponents to develop a "dump and chase" style of offence in the attacking zone?
A. The Boston Bruins
B. The Detroit Red Wings
C. The Chicago Blackhawks
D. The Toronto Maple Leafs

2.18 In NHL history how many goalies, if any, have ever been named team captain?
A. None
B. Three
C. Five
D. Six, each from an "Original Six" team

2.19 Who was the first blueliner to score 1,000 career points?
A. Bobby Orr
B. Paul Coffey
C. Denis Potvin
D. Larry Robinson

TEAM DEFENSE
Answers

2.1   **B. Buffalo's Dominik Hasek.**
If 1993–94 was the Year of the Goalie (and it was), then the Sabres' Hasek led the charge with his Vezina-winning year and breathtaking 1.95 GAA, the first average under the two-goals-per-game barrier in two decades since Parent (1.89 GAA) in 1973–74. To amass such a percentage, especially in today's higher scoring game, the 29-year-old Czech stood on his head while his teammates flooded the neutral zone in a retooled defense-oriented system that ran like clockwork after sniper Pat Lafontaine went down in December. The trap held opponents at bay and anybody breaking through was frequently frustrated by Hasek's anticipation and fleet-footed flamboyant style of netminding. Hasek posted 30–20–6 and seven shutouts on an paltry 28 shots per game average.

2.2   A. Ian Turnbull.

Four goals in one game by a defenseman was an NHL record that had been equalled six times but never broken in 60 years of hockey—until Turnbull shattered it, netting an unprecedented five goals in a Toronto 9–1 bombing of the Red Wings on February 2, 1977. No blueliner in NHL history has scored so often in a single-game performance, including defensive greats like Orr, Coffey or Day.

2.3   B. Tony Esposito.

Esposito earned "Tony O" in his first full NHL season, 1969–70, by zeroing Chicago's opponents a record 15 times in 63 games for a sizzling 2.17 GAA. For Esposito, that's a shutout almost every fourth start during his rookie year! More deserving than the nickname, Esposito won the Calder and Vezina Trophies and was named to the first All-Star team. Other rookies with double-digit shutout records are: Hainsworth (14) in 1926–27, Tiny Thompson (12) in 1928–29 and Sawchuk (11) in 1950–51. The Rangers' Mike Richter went without a shutout until his third NHL season.

2.4   B. Two times.

It has only happened twice in NHL history, and on both occasions to defensive stars. High-scoring defenseman Tom Anderson won league MVP in 1942, despite the Brooklyn Americans' seventh-place finish; and in 1954, Chicago goalie Al Rollins became just the second Hart winner from a last-place club after his Blackhawks finished with 12–51–7. Considering the lacklustre offense and porous defense he had in front of him, Rollins performed miracles to hold the goals against to 3.23, only one goal per game higher than the league average.

2.5 **C. Curtis Joseph.**
In 1993–94, Joseph established himself as the NHL's most overworked goaltender after facing a league record 2,382 shots while appearing in 71 games (36–23–11)—a 33.5 shots per game average. It broke the previous high mark, 2,202, again set by the St. Louis goalie in 1992–93. With backup Jon Casey now on the Blues roster, Joseph is catching less rubber and a well-deserved break.

2.6 **B. The Rangers' Sergei Zubov.**
Although many blueliners, including Leetch, Potvin and Bourque, have all led their team in season point totals, no defenseman has ever achieved it on a club finishing first overall. Not until 1993–94, when the Rangers were No. 1 and Zubov, who missed six games shuffling between Mike Keenan's doghouse and New York's Binghamton farm team, racked up 89 points to lead all Blueshirt point-getters (and all NHL defensemen with 77 assists). Teammates, impressed with his speed and puck handling, are already comparing the second-year D-man and 1994 Stanley Cup winner to all-star Islander Denis Potvin. In 1993–94 another record was set, both first *and* second place teams had defensemen as top scorers. Scott Stevens led all Devils with 78 points.

2.7 **C. Between 45 and 50 losses.**
Interesting, but a goalie record few netminders would brag about. Gary "Suitcase" Smith heads the stat box in this category.

THE TOP SINGLE-SEASON LOSING GOALIES

	Player	Team	Season	Losses
1	G. Smith	California	1970–71	48
2	A. Rollins	Chicago	1953–54	47
3	P. Sidorkiewicz	Ottawa	1992–93	46
4	H. Lumley	Chicago	1951–52	44
5	H. Lumley	Chicago	1950–51	41
6	C. Billington	Ottawa	1993–94	41

Current to 1993-94

2.8 **D. Bill Gadsby.**

Only about 25 NHL defensemen have had career totals that exceed 500 points, Gadsby being the first blueliner to reach that milestone in his 17th season on November 4, 1962 (against Chicago's Glenn Hall), only months ahead of Harvey, who notched his 500th point against his former club, the Canadiens, on February 6, 1963. Kelly, a defenseman in Detroit, was traded to Toronto (and moved to centre) before he could break the 500-point mark. Orr did it the fastest, amassing 500 points in under six seasons (1966–67 to 1971–72).

2.9 **C. Terry Sawchuk & Johnny Bower.**

In 1964, Sawchuk's Wings and Bower's Maple Leafs played an epic see-saw final series down to the seventh and deciding game. Bower shut out Detroit 4–0 to win the Cup, and that summer, after Sawchuk went unprotected, Leaf coach Punch Imlach astutely picked up the veteran. With 28 NHL years of experience between them, the old playoff adversaries stonewalled the league, winning the Vezina Trophy in 1965—the first time the trophy was shared under the two goalie system. It was Bower's second Vezina and Sawchuk's fourth.

2.10 B. The New Jersey Devils.

The Devils' 1993–94 turnaround, setting franchise records for victories (47) and points (106), can be attributable to the two-way defensive system employed by first-year head coach Jacques Lemaire, who brought the Montreal Canadiens' defense-oriented style of play to New Jersey and produced a roster of plus-only players. Under the tutelage of Lemaire and assistant coach Larry Robinson, blueliner Bruce Driver catapulted from a -10 in 1992–93 to a +29; Stephane Richer, a -1 to a +31; and, John McLean, a -6 to a +30. In all, seven regulars in the minus column jumped to plus figures (12 players over +20!); others, like Scott Stevens excelled from +14 to +53 (and led the NHL in plus/minus). Overall, the Devils cut down goals against, allowing 79 fewer goals than the previous season.

2.11 D. Five.

Bobby Orr, Denis Potvin, Paul Coffey, Al MacInnis and Brian Leetch are the only blueliners to record 100-point seasons in the NHL, each accomplishing the feat once except for Orr and Coffey, who did it multiple times during their careers. Orr had six consecutive 100-point seasons in Boston, while Coffey has recorded three in Edmonton and another two in Pittsburgh.

THE NHL'S FIVE DEFENSEMEN WITH 100-POINT SEASONS

Orr	TP	Coffey/TP		Potvin/TP		MacInnis/TP		Leetch/TP	
69–70	120	83–84	126	78–79	101	90–91	103	91–92	102
70–71	139	84–85	121						
71–72	117	85–86	138						
72–73	101	88–89	113						
73–74	122	89–90	103						
74–75	135								

Current to 1993–94

2.12 B. Terry Sawchuk.

Sawchuk recorded more shutouts (103) and won more games (435) than any other netminder in NHL history. Plante, who played 18 seasons, finished his NHL career with 434 wins, only one win less than Sawchuk's mark after 21 seasons. But include Plante's last pro season as a WHA Edmonton Oiler, where he won 15 matches, and the 1-2 standings reverse.

2.13 B. 50 to 100 goals.

The Canadiens knew what they were getting in 1970 when they assigned Butch Bouchard's son, Pierre, to their defense unit. Like father, like son. Both were big as redwoods. And both played in the same manner: low in goal production, tops in defensive skills. Bouchard the elder bluelined 15 seasons for Montreal, manhandling the opposition and steering away potential goals for Hab backstoppers Bill Durnan and Gerry McNeil; and the younger Bouchard duplicated his father's role for eight years with Ken Dryden, as a hard-nosed "defensive defenseman." Their stay-at-home gamemanship wasn't measured in goals but in quality of years'service. The Bouchards played 1,274 games and 189 playoff matches for a combined 79 goals in 23 seasons with the Canadiens.

2.14 A. Pierre Pilote.

Before Orr scored 64 points in 1968–69 to establish the new NHL season point total for defensemen, Chicago captain Pierre Pilote held the record with 59 points in 1964–65. Pilote, a three-time Norris Trophy winner and eight-time all-star, broke Babe Pratt's 21-year-old mark of 57 points set in 1943–44. Mohns, a sometimes-blueliner, wasn't playing rearguard in 1967–68, the season he scored 60 points on a line with Stan Mikita and Kenny Wharram. Kelly's highest season total as a defenseman was 54 points in 1950–51.

2.15 A. Gilles Meloche.

Meloche's 2,756 goals against over 18 NHL seasons far and away outdistances all other netminders, but that stat is deceiving. Meloche was better than most of the teams he backstopped, including the California Seals and Cleveland Barons. It began late in 1970 with Chicago, where he played just two games before the Seals trade. When California became Cleveland, later to merge with Minnesota, Meloche was still there, playing his best during the 1981 Stanley Cup finals between the North Stars and the Islanders. Meloche's last years were in Pittsburgh.

THE NHL'S MOST SCORED-UPON GOALIES						
Player	GP	W	L	T	GA	Avg.
1 G. Meloche	788	270	351	131	2756	3.64
2 T. Esposito	886	423	307	151	2563	2.92
3 G. Worsley	862	335	353	150	2432	2.90
4 T. Sawchuk	971	435	337	188	2401	2.52
5 R. Vachon	795	355	291	115	2310	2.99
6 G. Millen	604	215	284	89	2281	3.87
7 G. Hall	906	407	327	165	2239	2.51

2.16 B. Boston's Bobby Orr.

Although it's an accomplishment uncharacteristic of their playing position, a few defensemen have succeeded, including Desjardins, who became the first to score three goals in a Cup final game (1993) and Orr, the very first blueliner in NHL history to record a playoff hat trick. Orr did it on April 11, 1971 in a 5–2 Bruins' win at Montreal.

2.17 D. The Toronto Maple Leafs.

Under Jack Adams in the 1940s, the Wings became the first team to consistently shoot the puck into the opponent's end and chase it. The strategy was designed to counteract a defensive system made popular by Toronto coach Hap Day which allowed one man, the centre, to forecheck while the two wingers stayed back with the defensemen to pick up the attacking wingers. With four men guarding the Leaf blueline, it became impossible for any opposing centre to go up the middle with the puck and pass to a winger. So Detroit began dumping and chasing the puck into the attacking zone. Adams' "dump and chase" became an NHL standard; and Day, who bottled up the neutral zone, had developed the forerunner to today's trap play.

2.18 B. Three.

Montreal's George Hainsworth (1932–33) was the NHL's first goalie to wear the "C," followed the next year by Chicago's Charlie Gardiner (1933–34). The third and last goalie captain in the NHL was another Canadien, Bill Durnan (1948) who stepped into the captaincy for half a season after the career-ending injury to Toe Blake. In 1949–50, the League ruled goalies could no longer venture from their crease to argue calls, ending the brief and noble history of the goalie captain.

2.19 C. Denis Potvin.

Only three defensemen in NHL history have scored over 1,000 points. Potvin reached that scoring plateau first on April 4, 1987, followed by Coffey, on December 22, 1990 and Bourque, February 29, 1992. Neither Orr (915 pts.) nor Robinson (958 pts.) ever hit the 1,000-point mark.

GAME 2

TRASH TALK

It was not the most eloquent defense put forth by a hockey suit, but when Tom Reich, player agent to Mario Lemieux, blurted out to *The Hockey News'* Michael Ulmer: "If anybody thinks Mario is a whiner, they can kiss my ass in front of the Empire State Building," ah . . . it got the point across.

Trash talk is not strictly the preserve of on-ice mental pugilists. Here are some other hockey quotes (heard around and away from the rink) that whine with a little less bite. Match them to their *auteurs*.

(Solutions are on page 116)

Part 1

Cam Neely	Michael Eisner
Foster Hewitt	Jack Kent Cooke
Harold Ballard	Bobby Hull
	John Ziegler

1. _____ "If it ain't broke, why fix it?"
2. _____ "There are 200,000 Canadians in Southern California and I know why they moved here—they hate hockey."
3. _____ "They score! Henderson has scored for Canada!"
4. _____ "I wasn't sure about 50 shifts, let alone 50 goals."
5. _____ "I'm looking for guys you toss meat at and they go wild."

6. _____ "We made a movie called *The Mighty Ducks*. It did $50 million box office. That was our market research."

7. _____ "Brophy couldn't coach a dog in from a snow storm with a pork chop."

Part 2

Harry Neale	Gordie Howe
Al Iafrate	Alan Eagleson
Frank Griffiths, Sr.	Glenn Hall
Chris Pronger	Reporter Steve Simmons

1. _____ "I retired, not quit. I don't like the word quit."

2. _____ "Having a goal scored against you is like having your pants pulled down in front of 15,000 people."

3. _____ "Let's just get the two points."

4. _____ "You mean, I just take a cheque for $850,000 to my bank?"

5. _____ "Empty-net goals are for sissies."

6. _____ "I knew I was in trouble when I heard my best forward saying to my best defenseman, 'I always have a bad game when I hear that song,' and it was the national anthem."

7. _____ "We're not dealing with a series of Einsteins."

8. _____ "I want to hear Ed Belfour admit he let in a goal that was actually his fault. This guy would say he was screened on a penalty shot."

3

GREAT EXPECTATIONS

After the early rounds of most NHL drafts, GMs seldom expect to find players destined to make regular rotation on their club. Nevertheless, a surprising number of low picks have later turned up on NHL score sheets to become superstars, like Pavel Bure (113th), Doug Gilmour (134th), Brett Hull (117th) and Luc Robitaille (171st). Others, drafted high after careful scrutiny, have been equally unpredictable, sometimes firing blanks instead of bullets. Trades are just as quirky, giving managers licence for team-destruction as a result of a bad deal or, on occasion, adding just the right chemistry to produce a winner. Hey, this wheeling and dealing is part intuition, timing and luck—but never a science. Judge for yourself.

(*Answers are on page 36*)

3.1 **Who was the original No. 1 in the NHL draft?**
   A. Peter Mahovlich
   B. Walt McKechnie
   C. Orest Romashya
   D. Garry Monahan

3.2 **Who was the first U.S. college player drafted No. 1 overall?**
   A. Joe Juneau
   B. Pat LaFontaine
   C. Joe Murphy
   D. Brian Lawton

3.3 Which European club has had the most players drafted by the NHL?
A. Dynamo Moscow
B. Djurgarden Stockholm
C. Central Red Army (CSKA) Moscow
D. Dukia Jihlava, Czech Republic and Slovakia

3.4 Which brothers are the NHL's highest combined draft picks?
A. Sylvain and Pierre Turgeon
B. Ron and Rich Sutter
C. Scott and Rob Niedermayer
D. Eric and Brett Lindros

3.5 Who did the New York Rangers trade away to get Mark Messier?
A. Darren Turcotte, Brian Mullen and cash
B. Bernie Nicholls and two rookies
C. Two first-round draft choices and cash
D. Vincent Damphousse, minor leaguers and cash

3.6 Name the only year Quebec-born talent was chosen 1–2–3 in the Entry Draft?
A. 1971—Guy Lafleur's draft year
B. 1984—Mario Lemieux's draft year
C. 1987—Pierre Turgeon's draft year
D. 1993—Alexandre Daigle's draft year

3.7 Who is the youngest No. 1 overall pick?
A. Mike Modano
B. Dale Hawerchuk
C. Eric Lindros
D. Pierre Turgeon

3.8 Since 1980, which American college has produced the most NHL draft picks?
A. University of Minnesota
B. Boston University
C. Michigan State
D. University of Wisconsin

3.9 Who was the first big-name player signed by the WHA?
A. Gerry Cheevers
B. Bobby Hull
C. Derek Sanderson
D. Bernie Parent

3.10 Who was the first Russian ever selected in a first round of the NHL draft?
A. Alexei Kovalev
B. Pavel Bure
C. Viktor Kozlov
D. Alexei Yashin

3.11 What compensation, if any, did the Bruins receive from Chicago when Bobby Orr became a Blackhawk in 1976?
A. Nothing
B. Players
C. Cash
D. Future draft picks

3.12 What team(s) drafted the most Calder Trophy winners (rookies of the year)?
A. The Pittsburgh Penguins
B. The New York Islanders
C. The Calgary Flames
D. The Quebec Nordiques

3.13 Among these stars, pick the only player chosen in the NHL Entry Draft. (The other three were signed as free agents.)
A. Ed Belfour
B. Theoren Fleury
C. Mark Tinordi
D. Adam Oates

3.14 Which player, traded or acquired as a free-agent, has cost his new team the most first-round picks?
A. Wayne Gretzky
B. Scott Stevens
C. Eric Lindros
D. Kevin Stevens

3.15 How much did the New York Rangers pay the Buffalo Sabres in 1990 to acquire the rights to Ray Sheppard?
A. $1
B. $1,000
C. $10,000
D. $100,000

3.16 Which American high school has produced the most NHL draft picks?
A. Belmont Hill, MA
B. Mount St. Charles, RI
C. Edina, MN
D. Northwood Prep, NY

3.17 Which team has traded away the most first-round draft picks?
A. The St. Louis Blues
B. The Pittsburgh Penguins
C. The Los Angeles Kings
D. The Philadelphia Flyers

GREAT EXPECTATIONS
Answers

3.1 D. Garry Monahan.
The predecessor of today's Entry Draft was the NHL Amateur Draft, which when first held on June 5, 1963 drafted players of qualifying age (17 years and older), who were not already signed to NHL-sponsored junior clubs. Monahan, an unsigned 17-year-old winger playing for St. Michael's High School in Toronto, was picked first overall by Sam Pollock and Scotty Bowman of the Montreal Canadiens. With the $8,000 signing bonus Monahan was on his way. He bought himself a 1955 Chevy and within a few years the original No. 1 draft was playing in the big league, mostly with Toronto and Vancouver throughout the 1970s. He scored 285 points in 748 games and 12 NHL seasons. Mahovlich was picked second by Detroit, Romashya, third by Boston and McKechnie, sixth by Toronto.

3.2 C. Joe Murphy.
Murphy, a Canadian-born centre playing at Michigan State, was chosen first overall in 1986, the same year he won the Central Collegiate Hockey Association's Rookie of the Year honour. He was traded to Edmonton in 1989 and Chicago in February 1993 after a holdout. Murphy's best season was 1991–92 (35–47–82).

3.3 C. Central Red Army (CSKA) Moscow.
Among all European hockey teams, CSKA Moscow has proved the richest talent pool of NHL draftees, yielding 43 players since 1978, including Pavel Bure (1989), Alexander Mogilny (1988), Sergei Fedorov (1989) and four other Russians in 1994. CSKA's success at stocking such player calibre is based on the old Soviet hockey system which funnelled the very best players into the

Central Red Army team through military conscription, expressly to win world championships and Olympic gold medals. Today, the CIS system is "freer," other Russian teams now pay players and send them to university to avoid the army, or players soon leave to sign with the NHL. The European team with the next highest number of NHL draft picks (32) is Dynamo Moscow, the KGB-sponsored team.

3.4   A. Sylvain and Pierre Turgeon.
Sylvain (2nd overall by Hartford in 1983) and Pierre (1st overall by Buffalo in 1987) are the highest-drafted brothers in NHL history, followed by other sibling combos like the Niedermayers: Scott (3rd overall/New Jersey/1991) and Rob (5th overall/Florida/1993); the Sutters: Ron (4th overall/Flyers/1982) and Rich (10th overall/Pittsburgh/1982); and the Lindros clan: Eric (1st overall/Quebec/1991) and Brett (9th overall/Isles/1994).

3.5   B. Bernie Nicholls and two rookies.
Messier is that quality of athlete whose competitive spirit brings the most out of his peers. He is hockey's most formidable leader. Ranger GM Neil Smith knew it, too: "I don't think our franchise has ever had a player like him." Three seasons later, New York had their Stanley Cup. In retrospect, the trade was a steal, the Rangers giving up veteran centreman Nicholls and rookies Steve Rice and Louie DeBrusk to Edmonton. No cash was involved, according to NHL records.

3.6   A. 1971—Guy Lafleur's draft year.
The only year Quebec players swept the top three draft spots was in 1971 when Montreal picked Lafleur of the Quebec Remparts first, Detroit countered next by choosing Marcel Dionne of the St. Catherine Blackhawks and Vancouver selected Jocelyn Guevremont of the Junior Canadiens third.

3.7 D. Pierre Turgeon.

When Buffalo called Turgeon to the podium at the Joe Louis Arena in 1987, the Granby Bison was 17 years, 10 months old, the youngest-ever junior selected first overall in an NHL draft. Modano, Hawerchuk and Lindros were all 18-year-olds.

3.8 C. Michigan State.

Joe Murphy (1st overall/1986), Craig Simpson (2nd overall/1985) and Brian Smolinski (21st overall/1990) are all graduates of Michigan State's hockey program, one of America's most successful athletic programs, based on its leading 28 NHL picks drafted between 1980 and 1994. The University of Wisconsin has sent just 11 players to the draft tables since 1980, but players like Chris Chelios, Brian Mullen, Gary Suter, Pat Flatley and Tony Granato have well represented their alma mater in pro hockey.

3.9 D. Bernie Parent.

The WHA began signing NHL fringe players and minor leaguers in February 1972, the same month Parent inked his WHA contract with the Philadelphia Blazers. He soon quit the club because of contract problems and struck a deal with the Flyers, becoming the final major acquisition in Philadelphia's run at the Stanley Cup in 1974 and 1975. Hull signed his famous multi-million-dollar deal with the WHA Winnipeg Jets four months after Parent in June 1972.

3.10 A. Alexei Kovalev.

While Yashin (2nd overall/Ottawa/1992) and Oleg Tverdovsky (2nd overall/Florida/1994) are the highest-drafted Russians, Kovalev is the first player from the former Soviet Union picked in the first round, after being selected by the Rangers' GM Neil Smith 15th overall in 1991. Bure was Vancouver's fourth choice

(113th overall) in 1989 and Kozlov, San Josc's first pick (6th overall) in 1993.

3.11 A. Nothing.

On his last knees, Orr signed with Chicago, after, unbeknownst to him, his agent Alan Eagleson turned down two Bruin contract offers (including the famous 18.5% team ownership deal) that would have kept the all-star defenseman in Boston. Instead, Orr unhappily left the Bruins and became a Blackhawk for a $3-million-dollar, six-year package, without compensation to Boston. The deal was struck just two months before the NHL's new Collective Bargaining Agreement, which included a provision for team compensation. The Bruins challenged the Blackhawks in federal court on compensation and tampering charges but the case was dismissed by a Chicago judge. The deal is the only one of its kind involving a player of Orr's stature that went without some form of compensation.

3.12 B and C. The New York Islanders & The Calgary Flames.

The Islanders, perhaps victimized by their own early success, have not picked a rookie of the year since the 1970s when they selected three Calder winners—Denis Potvin (1974), Bryan Trottier (1976) and Mike Bossy (1978)—in a five-year span. Calgary, too, has a nose for choosing rookies who win the Calder. Three current or former Flames—Gary Suter (1986), Joe Nieuwendyk (1988) and Sergei Makarov (1990)—have won rookie honours. More exceptional, none of Calgary's picks were first-rounders. Nieuwendyk went 27th (2nd round/1985), Suter, 180th (9th round/1984) and Makarov, 231st (12th round/1983). Under previous ownership in Atlanta, the Flames had another two Calder winners in Eric Vail (1975) and Willi Plett (1977).

3.13 B. Theoren Fleury.

"Better late than never" does not apply to this group of NHL stars. While each have become dominant players on their respective teams, Fleury alone was drafted and, at that, a late pick (166th in 1987). The other greats went undrafted (!): Belfour was signed by Chicago in 1987; Tinordi, by the Rangers (1987); and Oates, by Detroit (1985).

3.14 B. Scott Stevens.

There was no spirit in St. Louis after the Blues forfeited an unprecedented five number-one picks to the Washington Capitals for signing free agent Stevens in 1990. Worse, the Blues not only gave up first rounders in 1991, 1992, 1993, 1994 and 1995 for the All-Star defenseman, but Stevens played just 78 games (5–44–49) in 1990–91 before being sent to New Jersey for compensation when the Blues signed free agent Brendan Shanahan.

3.15 A. $1.

Sheppard's 52-goal season in 1993-94 had a few NHL managers shaking their heads, particularly those who passed up Buffalo's one-dollar price tag for the heavy-footed winger. The Rangers went "daaah" too, not knowing what to do with Sheppard before releasing him to sign as a free agent with Detroit, the team that found the right combination of linemates to produce the "one-dollar" 50-goal scorer. Sheppard now earns $800,000 per annum.

3.16 D. Northwood Prep, NY.

Since 1980, players like Brian Leetch, Keith Tkachuk, Jeremy Roenick and Tom Barrasso have all been drafted directly from U.S. high schools. Northwood Prep in New York has produced the highest number of NHL prospects, 19 students drafted, including Mike Richter

(28th overall/1985) and Jim Campbell (28th over-
all/1991). Edina in Minnesota runs second with 16
draftees, such as Paul Ranheim and David Maley.

3.17   C. The Los Angeles Kings.
St. Louis's reputation for building teams by trading
away first rounders (and through free-agent signings)
is no secret, but the Kings have done it more often and
with far greater panache (translation: reckless aban-
don). Although the Blues forfeited 13 number-one picks
since 1969, Los Angeles traded away its first choice in
1969, 1970, 1971, 1972, 1973, 1974, 1975, 1976, 1977,
1978, 1982, 1983, 1989, 1991, 1992 and 1993—a stagger-
ing 16 times. They did acquire Wayne Gretzky for three
top picks (players and big cash) but got fleeced on
almost every other deal involving first-round picks.
Players like Ray Bourque, Steve Shutt, Ron Duguay,
Mario Tremblay, Pierre Mondou, Reggie Leach, Phil
Housley and Tom Barrasso were all first-rounders other
teams drafted in the position the Kings dealt away. In
return, Los Angeles picked up stiffs like Skip Krake,
Gerry Desjardins, Gene Carr and Glenn Goldup. Even
when they traded first-round positions with Chicago in
1984, the Hawks got Ed Olczyk (originally an L.A. pick)
and the Kings took Craig Redmond. Unfortunately, St.
Louis will catch up to Los Angeles. The Blues haven't
selected a top pick since 1989 and won't have another
until 1996 thanks in part to the Scott Stevens compensation debacle. Pittsburgh has given up eight first-
rounders.

GAME 3

THE TOP EXPANSION PICKS

Match the NHL expansion teams in the left column with their very first draft picks in the right column. The bracketed draft positions after the player's names could help in your selections.

(Solutions are on page 116)

1. ____ Buffalo (1970)   A. Pat Falloon (2nd)

2. ____ Vancouver (1970)   B. Paul Kariya (4th)

3. ____ Islanders (1972)   C. Kevin Lowe (21st)

4. ____ Atlanta (1972)   D. Dale Tallon (2nd)

5. ____ Washington (1974)   E. Jimmy Mann (19th)

6. ____ Kansas City (1974)   F. Gilbert Perreault (1st)

7. ____ Hartford (1979)   G. Jacques Richard (2nd)

8. ____ Winnipeg (1979)   H. Roman Hamrlik (1st)

9. ____ Quebec (1979)   I. Rob Niedermayer (5th)

10. ____ Edmonton (1979)   J. Wilf Paiement (2nd)

11. ____ San Jose (1991)   K. Ray Allison (18th)

12. ____ Tampa Bay (1992)   L. Michel Goulet (20th)

13. ____ Ottawa (1992)   M. Greg Joly (1st)

14. ____ Anaheim (1993)   N. Alexei Yashin (2nd)

15. ____ Florida (1993)   O. Billy Harris (1st)

4

WHO AM I?

Who is the only hockey player to win a Canada Cup, Stanley Cup and World Championship? In this chapter we take a break from our usual line of questioning and force you to go it alone without multiple-choice alternatives. To assist you, the year it happened is included. For example, our first answer (from above) is a Canadian goalie who won this triple crown of hockey in 1990, 1991 and 1994. Give up? Edmonton's Bill Ranford is the only player ever to win the Stanley Cup (1990), Canada Cup (1991) and World Championship (1994).

(Answers are on page 45)

4.1   I am the last NHLer to play without a helmet. I played in 1993 94. *Who am I?*

4.2   I am the first underage European to sign a North American professional contract. I played in the International Hockey League at 17 years old in 1993–94. *Who am I?*

4.3   I gave up Mike Gartner's 100th, 200th and 300th goals while goaltending for three different clubs. It happened between 1981 and 1987. *Who am I?*

4.4   I am the first and only NHLer to captain two different teams to the Stanley Cup. *Who am I?* (Sorry, if we gave the years, this would be a no-brainer.)

4.5 I was the last Blackhawk to leave the ice after Chicago Stadium's final NHL game. It happened in 1994. *Who am I?*

4.6 I was the first player credited with raising his stick to signal the scoring of a goal after the NHL initiated a mandatory policy instituting this practice in 1947. *Who am I?*

4.7 I was the first NHLer to have a penalty shot in overtime in the regular season. It happened in 1989. *Who am I?*

4.8 After Wayne Gretzky, I am (with Mario Lemieux) the second fastest NHLer to score 50 goals in a season. It happened in 1993–94. *Who am I?*

4.9 I played every minute of every playoff game with the Montreal Canadiens during their record five consecutive championships from 1956 through 1960. *Who am I?*

4.10 I am the first American to capture the Conn Smythe Trophy as playoff MVP. It happened in 1994. *Who am I?*

4.11 In the dying moments of game eight of the 1972 Canada-Soviet Summit Series, I was called off the ice by Paul Henderson, who replaced me and scored the series-winning goal. *Who am I?*

4.12 I am the last NHLer to score 50 goals (in one season) without a helmet. It happened in 1982–83. *Who am I?*

4.13 I have the dubious honour of being the first NHL goalie who Wayne Gretzky scored a goal on, and 15 years later I played a role in his record 802nd tally. It happened in 1979 and 1994. *Who am I?*

4.14 After the Rangers won the 1994 Stanley Cup and ended their 54-year drought, another team now takes over as the league's most dormant Stanley Cup winner. We haven't won in 40 years. *Who Are We?*

WHO AM I?
Answers

4.1 **Craig MacTavish**, who signed a player's contract prior to the 1979 cutoff date for exemption of the NHL's helmet rule, is the last helmetless NHLer. Although the league reversed this rule in 1992, permitting players to go bareheaded, none have done so on a permanent basis.

4.2 In 1993, when he signed with the IHL's Las Vegas Thunder, **Radek Bonk** was 17, a fresh-faced centre from Koprivnice in the Czech Republic. Because of his age, many expected a difficult adjustment in a man's pro league, but Bonk, who earned $100,000, proved his big-league skills by scoring 42 goals and 87 points in 76 games with the Thunder. Bonk was Ottawa's first choice, third overall in the 1994 NHL Entry Draft.

4.3 It seemed whenever Gartner set a personal record, **Glen Hanlon** was his fall guy, backstopping the wrong team at the wrong time on the wrong goal. On the night Gartner celebrated his 100th, Hanlon was his Canuck target; his 200th, Hanlon let it slip by as a Ranger; and his 300th, again Hanlon outdid himself, this time in a Red Wing uniform.

4.4   **Mark Messier** captained both the Stanley Cup champion 1990 Edmonton Oilers and the 1994 New York Rangers.

4.5   On April 28, 1994, just moments after the ceremonial handshakes to end the Conference quarterfinals and the Hawks playoff hopes, **Jeremy Roenick** circled the ice, waved to Chicago fans and tossed his stick into the stands, saying goodbye forever to the 65-year-old home of the Blackhawks. He was the last Hawk to skate in Chicago Stadium before the club moved into the United Center in 1994–95.

4.6   It was an idea proposed by Frank Patrick (who was the guiding force behind many of hockey's early innovations including the penalty shot, the blue line and the first playoff system in any sport) and first tried on November 13, 1947, when Chicago's **Billy Reay** raised his stick on purpose after scoring a goal against the Canadiens. No doubt players before him had celebrated a goal in a similar manner, but Reay was the first scorer to officially do it under a mandatory policy initiated in 1947 and approved by league president Clarence Campbell.

4.7   After being hauled down on a breakaway on February 2, 1989, **Luc Robitaille** is awarded the NHL's first penalty shot in regular season overtime. But a rolling puck on bad ice forced the Kings sniper to shoot quickly, missing the Devils' half-open net and hitting a flopping Sean Burke on the shoulder.

4.8   **Cam Neely** blazed through the NHL in 1993–94 on the comeback trail that netted the power forward 50 goals in 44 games, tying Lemieux's 50-in-44 mark from 1988-89; only Gretzky is ahead with 50-in-39 and 50-in-42 in 1981–82 and 1983–84 respectively.

4.9 Obviously, the only player to play every minute of every playoff game could be the goaltender, **Jacques Plante**, one of just 12 Canadiens who appeared in all five straight Stanley Cups.

4.10 **Brian Leetch**, from Corpus Christi, Texas, is the first American-born NHLer to win the Conn Smythe, capturing the playoff MVP award in 1994 and leading all post-season scorers with 34 points.

4.11 Henderson admits he's never called another player off the ice before or after, but, at the time, he felt he could score the winning goal. Not just a heroic notion, considering Henderson already had two previous game winners in Russia. Fortunately, **Pete Mahovlich,** on a line with Phil Esposito and Yvan Cournoyer, gave Henderson the nod and, with 34 seconds left on the clock, he roofed a shot heard 'round the world past a sprawling Vladislav Tretiak to win the final game 6–5 and the first-ever Canada-Soviet series, 4–3–1.

4.12 Although dozens of NHLers signed the exemption clause allowing them to play helmetless, no bareheaded player managed a 50-goal season after 1982–83, the year Chicago's **Al Secord** scored 54 goals without protective headgear.

4.13 The Canucks' **Glen Hanlon**, who will forever be remembered as Gretzky's "first," was also the goaltending coach for Vancouver, the team Gretzky scored No. 802 against.

4.14 The **Detroit Red Wings**, winners of seven Stanley Cups, the most of any American team, last won the championship in 1955—40 long Cup-less years and counting.

GAME 4

THE CROSSNUMBER

(Solution is on page 117)

Across
1. No. of Maple Leaf Cups
3. Gretzky's playoff career goals
4. Year Toronto won 1st of 3 Cups
7. Year Blackhawks last won Cup
9. Craig Janney's uniform no.
10. Most consecutive games by goalie
11. Fewest games Bobby Hull needed to score 50 goals
13. Most NHL seasons, Gordie Howe
14. Most Shark losses '92-93
15. Official capacity of MSG
16. 1st year Vezina Trophy awarded
18. Esposito's best season point totals
19. Geoff Courtnall's uniform no.
21. Punch Imlach's favourite number
22. Rookie goal total, Nieuwendyk
24. Best yr. assist total, Gretzky
26. Most pro seasons, Gordie Howe
28. Martin Brodeur's uniform no.
29. Orr's original signing bonus
30. Nels Stewart's career goals
31. Gretzky's best season point total
33. Most power play goals in yr.
35. Howe's age/best season '68–69
36. Year Rangers won Cup at MSG
37. Rookie goal total Mario
38. Best rookie goal total/playoffs
39. Most season goals by left winger, Luc Robitaille
40. Most home wins one yr., Flyers
41. Most assists one season
43. Minute total of longest game ever
44. NHL record, most shots one yr.
45. Sergei Fedorov's uniform no.
46. 50-in-_____
47. Official capacity of Boston Garden
49. Fewest no. of goals against in one season, Toronto & Montreal
52. Cost of joining league in 1967
53. Average player salary in 1989
54. Scoreless tie
55. Most goals by D-man, playoff yr.
57. Bobby Hull's slapshot speed
58. Most PIM one yr., Sabres
61. Most games appeared in by goalie
62. Official capacity of ThunderDome
63. Typical cost of a dasher board advertisement

Down
1. Year Red Wings won 1st Cup
2. Most short-handed goals one yr.
3. Official capacity Joe Louis Arena
4. Yr. of Richard's 500th goal
5. Rookie goal total, Eric Lindros
6. Top player salary in 1932
8. Off. capacity Maple Leaf Gardens
12. Most SOs one yr., Hainsworth
13. Most ties one season, Flyers
15. Attendance, 1st game at MLG
16. No. of games it took Howe to break Richard's 544-goal record
17. Most games one yr. by goalie
18. Wendel Clark's uniform no.
20. Salary Howe made in 1968
23. Off. capacity of Montreal Forum
24. Most assists one yr. by Orr
25. Brian Skrudland's uniform no.
27. Most Cups, Canadiens
30. Most PIM, Tiger Williams
31. Sergei Zubov's uniform no.
32. Yr. Gretzky scored 500th goal
33. No. CDN homes with TV in 1951
34. Teemu Selanne's uniform no.
35. Most goals one team one season
38. Doug Gilmour's TP in 1993–94
40. Mike Richter's uniform no.
42. $ CBS paid for NHL Game of the Week in 1966–67
43. Yr. Richard scored 50-in-50
44. Most goals by Bobby Hull, one yr.
46. Break-even percentage
47. Yr. of no Stanley Cup winner
48. Howe's NHL career goal total
49. Most team scoring TP one yr.
50. Longest road loss streak, Ottawa
51. Howe's NHL point total
52. Rookie PIM of Lou Fontinato
56. Scott Niedermayer's uniform no.
59. Rod Brind'Amour's uniform no.
60. Most power play Gs playoff career

48

5

ALL IN THE FAMILY

Team achievements are a synergistic endeavour. To excel, players must play for each other, rather than for themselves. More than just snipers depending on playmakers for the pass or goalies counting on their rearguard, on successful clubs, offense can be dictated by rushing defensemen and point men pinching in the attack; and defence has become every player's job the moment the opposition takes the puck. In this chapter on team performance, its "one for all and all for one."

(Answers are on page 53)

5.1 **Which NHL team has the oldest name in hockey?**
A. Toronto—The Maple Leafs
B. Ottawa—The Senators
C. Boston—The Bruins
D. Montreal—The Canadiens

5.2 **Which team recorded the NHL's greatest point increase in a single-season turnaround?**
A. The San Jose Sharks in 1993–94
B. The New York Islanders in 1974–75
C. The Boston Bruins in 1967–68
D. The Quebec Nordiques in 1992–93

5.3 **Which expansion team was first to produce an Art Ross Trophy winner as the league's leading scorer?**
A. The Los Angeles Kings
B. The Edmonton Oilers
C. The New York Islanders
D. The Philadelphia Flyers

5.4 Which minor pro city has the greatest average attendance for hockey games?
A. Milwaukee
B. Oklahoma City
C. Providence
D. Cincinnati

5.5 Who coached the most consecutive years with one team?
A. Detroit's Jack Adams
B. Montreal's Dick Irvin
C. Chicago's Billy Reay
D. The Islanders' Al Arbour

5.6 Which NHL team set the NHL's all-time attendance record in 1993–94?
A. The Detroit Red Wings
B. The Tampa Bay Lightning
C. The Calgary Flames
D. The New York Rangers

5.7 Name the only NHL team in history to place its players first, second, third and fourth in the scoring race in the same season.
A. The Pittsburgh Penguins
B. The Montreal Canadiens
C. The Edmonton Oilers
D. The Boston Bruins

5.8 What team wears patches on their sweaters bearing the insignia "2 Pts. F.G."?
A. The San Jose Sharks
B. The Calgary Flames
C. The Vancouver Canucks
D. The Florida Panthers

5.9 Which head coach (minimum 600 NHL games) has been behind the bench with the most teams?
A. Jacques Demers
B. Mike Keenan
C. Roger Neilson
D. Scotty Bowman

5.10 Name the last NHL team to cease operations, thereby reducing the league to the "Original Six" clubs in 1942-43.
A. The Montreal Maroons
B. The Ottawa Senators
C. The Vancouver Millionaires
D. The Brooklyn Americans

5.11 Which expansion team scored the most goals in its first NHL season?
A. The Florida Panthers in 1993–94
B. The Hartford Whalers in 1979–80
C. The Edmonton Oilers in 1979–80
D. The Tampa Bay Lightning in 1992–93

5.12 All six Sutter brothers from Viking, Alberta played for the same WHL junior team. Which club?
A. The Medicine Hat Tigers
B. The Red Deer Rebels
C. The Moose Jaw Warriors
D. The Lethbridge Broncos

5.13 What did players on the Montreal Canadiens wear in a pre-game warm-up in 1948 to show support for their coach Dick Irvin?
A. Red fedoras
B. Leather helmets
C. Stanley Cup rings
D. Black arm bands

5.14 How many games, if any, in NHL history have been played to both a scoreless and penalty-free decision?
   A. Only one game
   B. Five games
   C. Ten games
   D. It has never happened.

5.15 From what historical reference did Calgary get their team name?
   A. The original name of Calgary's first professional hockey team in the 1920s
   B. The legacy of the rich oil-producing fields of Alberta
   C. The nickname of ex-owner Nelson Skalbania's air force squadron
   D. The burning of Atlanta during America's Civil War

5.16 Which NHL team is the first to employ a hyperbaric oxygen chamber?
   A. The New York Rangers
   B. The Los Angeles Kings
   C. The Vancouver Canucks
   D. The Toronto Maple Leafs

ALL IN THE FAMILY
Answers

5.1 **B. Ottawa—The Senators.**
The Senators' origins are rooted in the Ottawa City Hockey Club, which began playing the game around 1884. Fondly remembered as the Silver Seven, the Senators won three Stanley Cups between 1903 and 1906 and again in 1908–09. The following season,

1909–10, Montreal joined the National Hockey Association, the predecessor to the NHL, and called themselves the Canadiens. In North American professional sports, Major League Baseball's Phillies (1883) and the National Football League's Cardinals (1899) have older names.

5.2   A. The San Jose Sharks in 1993-94.
The three-year-old Sharks went from being the second-worst NHL team (24 points), losing 71 games in 1992–93, to playoff contenders the next year, 1993–94, finishing eighth (82 points) in the Western Conference—a 58-point turnaround and a league record. Their playoff drive, upsetting the heavily favoured Red Wings and pushing Toronto to the brink in game seven, proved the potency of the new Shark attack. Was it the new stadium? The new coach, Kevin Constantine? Or the new system? To say nothing of the spectacular play of Arturs Irbe and Soviet veterans Igor Larionov and Sergei Makarov, who found their wheels while helping the Sharks achieve respectability. The previous record turnaround was 52 points, held by the 1992–93 Nordiques.

5.3   C. The New York Islanders.
In 1978–79, Bryan Trottier, the scrappy star centre with the Islanders, scored 134 points (four more than the Kings' Marcel Dionne) to become the first player from an expansion team to win the NHL's scoring race. Trottier doubled his fortune, winning not only the Art Ross but the Hart Trophy as league MVP.

5.4   B. Oklahoma City.
It's not NHL-calibre hockey, but there's a minor pro boom going on in America and it's taking off in places like Las Vegas, Peoria and Kalamazoo. About 70 teams employing 1,200 players in six leagues criss-cross the continent, attracting respectable crowds of five or six

thousand per game. Although the International Hockey League has the best attendance averages among seven of the top 12 minor pro teams and highest attendance overall league-wise, Oklahoma City in the Central Hockey League leads all minor league clubs, averaging 10,438 fans per home game. Milwaukee (9,509 fans), Providence (9,203 fans) and South Carolina (9,151 fans) have the next best hockey attendance averages on the circuit.

5.5 A. Detroit's Jack Adams.

Known as "Mr. Detroit Red Wings," Adams managed the organization for 35 years, coaching 20 uninterrupted seasons (1927 to 1946) and compiling a win/tie point percentage of .512 on 964 games (413–390–161). He won three Stanley Cups as coach, including back-to-back in 1936 and 1937, the first time an American team took two straight championships. Under Adams's reign as club manager, the Red Wings won a total of 12 league titles and four more Stanley Cups before his retirement in 1963. His greatest personal achievement was the development of Gordie Howe. Today, the NHL honours its coach of the year with the Jack Adams Award.

	THE NHL'S TOP SIX IRONMEN COACHES				
Years	Coach	Team	Seasons	Games	%
20	Jack Adams	Detroit	1927 to 1947	964	.512
15	Dick Irvin	Montreal	1940 to 1955	896	.566
14	Billy Reay	Chicago	1963 to 1977	1012	.589
13	*Al Arbour	Islanders	1973 to 1986	1038	.613
13	Toe Blake	Montreal	1955 to 1968	914	.634
13	Les Patrick	Rangers	1926 to 1939	604	.554

* *Arbour coached the Islanders again from 1988 to 1994*

5.6 A. The Detroit Red Wings.

In each of its 41 home games in 1993–94, the Red Wings filled Joe Louis Arena to 100% capacity drawing a single-season attendance record of 812,640 fans or 19,820 per game. That figure broke the previous NHL all-time high average of 19,723, set by Detroit in 1991–92. Had the Lightning not played five games in Orlando (which averaged only 10,068 per game), they would have exceeded Detroit's record high after averaging 20,988 in the 28,000-seat ThunderDome. The aggregate average of 19,656 gave Tampa Bay (805,904) the runner-up position, while Calgary (792,307) and New York (738,330) placed next best.

5.7 D. The Boston Bruins.

The Bruins of the 1970s made the NHL scoring totals their own personal race for six seasons from 1969 to 1975, each year Phil Esposito and Bobby Orr alternated first and second positions (except 1972–73), and twice four Boston players hogged the top four spots, 1970–71 and 1973–74.

THE BOSTON BRUINS SCORING RAMPAGE							
1970–71				*1973–74*			
Player	G	A	PTS	Player	G	A	PTS
1 P. Esposito	76	76	152	1 P. Esposito	68	77	145
2 B. Orr	37	102	139	2 B. Orr	32	90	122
3 J. Bucyk	51	65	116	3 K. Hodge	50	55	105
4 K. Hodge	43	62	105	4 W. Cashman	30	59	89
5 B. Hull	44	52	96	5 B. Clarke	35	52	87
6 N. Ullman	34	51	85	6 R. Martin	52	34	86

5.8 C. The Vancouver Canucks.

In honour of the late Frank Griffiths, Sr., the man considered to have saved hockey in Vancouver when he bought the financially failing club in 1974, the Canucks wear "2 Pts. F.G." patches, a team epitaph for Griffiths's favourite expression, "Let's just get the two points." Griffiths is a member of the Hockey Hall of Fame.

5.9 C. Roger Neilson.

From Toronto (1977–79) to Buffalo (1980–81) to Vancouver (1982–84) to Los Angeles (1984) to New York (1989–93) to Florida (1993–), Neilson's six head coaching assignments tops all others, including Bowman's five stops. Neilson began his NHL coaching career under Harold Ballard in Toronto, peaked in Vancouver during the Cup finals against the Islanders, dived in New York after messing with Mark Messier and rose again in Florida, when the Panthers almost became the first expansion team to make the playoffs in their inaugural season. Neilson also co-coached in Chicago under Bob Pulford for two seasons (1985 to 1987).

5.10 D. The Brooklyn Americans.

The Amerks, with their famous stars-and-stripes jerseys, were New York's first hockey team and starred hockey greats like "Bullet" Joe Simpson, Lionel Conacher and Roy Worters. Plugging away in the Broadway shadow of Lester Patrick's New York Rangers, however, the Americans could do little to win fans or hockey games. The club even changed its name from the "New York Americans" to the "Brooklyn Americans." But the losses continued, especially after the financially troubled franchise dealt away its stars for cash and younger players. By 1942, the Americans were forced to cease operations, reducing the NHL to a six-team league.

5.11 B. The Hartford Whalers in 1979-80.

It shouldn't be too surprising that the Whalers lead all NHL expansion teams in the goals scored column. Playing alongside veterans like Gordie and Mark Howe, Dave Keon and Bobby Hull, Hartford had two

100-point players in Mike Rogers and Blaine Stoughton. In the 80-game schedule, the Whalers averaged 3.79 goals per game or 303 goals, edging the Gretzky-led Oilers (301 goals). The Panthers had 233 goals and the Lightning 245 goals in 84 games.

5.12 D. The Lethbridge Broncos.

From 1974 through 1983 the Broncos always had at least one of six Sutter brothers in uniform racking up points, roughing up opponents or killing off penalties. In nine seasons they combined to play 781 games, score 1,007 points and amass 2,248 penalty minutes. Lethbridge is about 200 miles south of the Sutters' home in Viking, Alberta.

5.13 A. Red fedoras.

Mired in a season-long slump, the Canadiens wore bright red fedoras at a 1948 practice after an angry Montreal fan made newspaper headlines by threatening to burn down the Forum if Irvin remained coach. The story broke while the team was in Toronto, so during the pre-game skate at Maple Leaf Gardens, the Canadiens wore the fireman-like red hats and pointed their sticks as if they were fire hoses. The theatrics took a little heat off the team, but the Canadiens still finished in fifth place with Irvin as coach. The Forum went unscathed.

5.14 A. Only one game.

If baseball has its dog-days of summer, then hockey has the February blahs, when teams are drudging through the long schedule still more than a month away from the playoffs. So it stands to reason that the lone "stats-free" game in NHL history happened on February 20th, 1944, in an undistinguished performance by the Hawks and the Maple Leafs, who could manage neither a goal nor even a penalty. The game was played in under two hours with little excitement except for a nullified goal, called back on a high stick. Bill Chadwick was the referee.

5.15 D. The burning of Atlanta during America's Civil War.

When Calgary was awarded the old Atlanta franchise in 1980, it retained the "Flames" name and its historical inspiration, the capture and burning of Atlanta by General Sherman's Union forces in 1864. Almost the entire Georgia capital was lost before the flames were extinguished. In hockey, the NHL survived for eight seasons in Atlanta and, much like baseball's old New York Giants and Brooklyn Dodgers, the Flames' new owners felt the team's original name and logo were strong enough to represent Calgary's entry into the NHL. In 1980, the logo's fiery "A" became a flaming "C."

5.16 C. The Vancouver Canucks.

The Canucks are considered the first professional sports team in North America to use a hyperbaric oxygen therapy unit, but judging by their gritty playoff performance in 1994's Stanley Cup finals (losing in game seven, 3–2), wider acceptance is only a matter of time. Used mainly in deep-sea diving and space exploration, the pressurized chamber pumps high doses of oxygen through a mask to the patient locked inside. The pressure, about twice normal, permits absorption of oxygen into the plasma at 15 times its usual rate. The much-needed oxygen increases the healing process in injuries and keeps swelling to a minimum. Players report the therapy unit also helps relieve body strain.

The honour of wearing the team "C" is not a title bestowed on just any player. It's given careful consideration, often beyond the scoring abilities and defensive attributes of even the best players. Leadership, attitude and maturity are the most important qualifications in the choice of captain, both on-ice and off-ice, where he bears the responsibility of team representative between players and coaches.

Thirty-two captains, listed below, appear in the puzzle, horizontally, vertically, diagonally or backwards. Some are easily found, like Pat Quinn, one-time captain of the Atlanta Flames; others require a more careful search. After you've circled all 32 names, read the remaining letters in descending order to spell a one-time "no-frills" captain of the Montreal Canadiens.

(Solutions are on page 117)

ABEL	DELVECCHIO	PERREAULT
APPS	KEON	PILOTE
BERENSON	KINDRACHUK	PRONOVOST
BRIDGMAN	KURTENBACH	QUINN
BUCYK	LABRE	RISEBROUGH
CARBONNEAU	LAFONTAINE	RUSKOWSKI
CASHMAN	MAGNUSON	SCHMIDT
CHRISTIAN	MCDONALD	SHMYR
CONACHER	NIEUWENDYK	VASKO
COURNOYER	PAIEMENT	WESTFALL
DAY	PARK	

GAME 5

THE NHL CAPTAINS

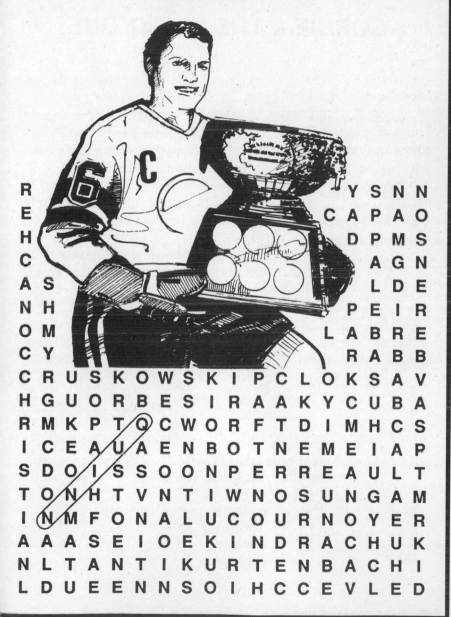

```
R                                           Y S N   N
E H                                       C A P A   O
H C                                       D P M S   N
C A       S                               A G N     E
A N       H                               L D       E
N O       M                               P E I R   R
O C       Y                               L A B R   E
C C   R U S K O W S K I   P C L O K S A V
C H G U O R B E S I R A A K Y C U B A
H R M K P T Q C W O R F T D I M H C S
R I C E A U A E N B O T N E M E I A P
I S D O I S S O O N P E R R E A U L T
S T O N H T V N T I W N O S U N G A M
T I N M F O N A L U C O U R N O Y E R
I A A A S E I O E K I N D R A C H U K
A N L T A N T I K U R T E N B A C H I
N L D U E E N N S O I H C C E V L E D
```

6

GORDIE & THE GREAT ONE

Gordie Howe and Wayne Gretzky met for the first time at a Kiwanis award banquet when young Gretzky was an 11-year-old wonder kid playing Pee Wee hockey in Brantford, Ontario. The previous year, Wayne created national attention after scoring 378 goals in 69 games (and winning the scoring race by 238 goals). Only four foot four, he was already dubbed the Great Gretzky. Howe's advice that night in 1972? "Practice your backhand, kid. It's an important shot."

Sure enough, Gretzky's first WHA and NHL goals were scored on the backhand. And when he tied and broke Howe's 1,850 NHL/career-point total, again backhanders were his weapon of choice. As scoring champs, Gretzky and Howe share few parallels; it's an almost impossible comparison considering the pair played different styles of hockey in different eras. But both became the league's most formidable offensive stars—the only NHLers to score more than 800 regular season goals.

(Answers are on page 66)

6.1 **How many goals did Wayne Gretzky score as an Oiler versus as a King to reach his NHL record 802-goal mark?**
   A. 483 (Oilers) + 319 (Kings) = 802
   B. 503 (Oilers) + 299 (Kings) = 802
   C. 543 (Oilers) + 259 (Kings) = 802
   D. 583 (Oilers) + 219 (Kings) = 802

6.2 How many professional hockey games did Gordie Howe play in during his 32-year career?
A. Between 1,500 and 1,800 games
B. Between 1,800 and 2,100 games
C. Between 2,100 and 2,400 games
D. More than 2,400 games

6.3 Which goalie did Wayne Gretzky beat to break Gordie Howe's NHL 801-goal record?
A. Arturs Irbe
B. Kirk McLean
C. Chris Osgood
D. Mike Vernon

6.4 Which team was Gordie Howe playing with when he scored his 1,000th professional goal in regular season and playoff action?
A. The Detroit Red Wings
B. The Houston Aeros
C. The New England Whalers
D. The Hartford Whalers

6.5 Which goalie gave up the most of Wayne Gretzky's 802 goals?
A. Richard Brodeur
B. Greg Millen
C. Kirk McLean
D. Mike Liut

6.6 What was Gordie Howe's "biggest thrill in hockey?"
A. Becoming the first 50 year-old to score an NHL goal
B. Playing alongside both Maurice Richard and Wayne Gretzky in All-Star games during his 32-year career
C. Playing alongside his sons, Mark and Marty
D. His front office job with the Red Wings

6.7 What is Walter Gretzky's nickname for his son Wayne?
A. Gretz
B. Wiener
C. Wayne-o
D. Wayner

6.8 How many times, if any, did Gordie Howe score 50 or more goals in an NHL or WHA season?
A. Only once
B. Two times
C. Three times
D. It never happened.

6.9 In number of games, what is the NHL's longest consecutive point-scoring streak? (And who did it?)
A. Between 35 and 40 games
B. Between 40 and 45 games
C. Between 45 and 50 games
D. More than 50 games

6.10 How many times, if any, did Howe and Gretzky play together on the same team?
A. Three times
B. Seven times
C. 11 times
D. It never happened.

6.11 How many NHL games did it take Wayne Gretzky to score 500 goals?
A. 575
B. 600
C. 625
D. 650

6.12 What NHL scoring record does Gordie Howe still hold?
   A. Most three-or-more goal games
   B. Most 20-or-more goal seasons
   C. Most 30-or-more goal seasons
   D. Most assists, including playoffs

6.13 In his 802-goal career record how many empty net goals has Wayne Gretzky scored?
   A. 20 to 30
   B. 30 to 40
   C. 40 to 50
   D. More than 50

6.14 How long was Gordie Howe's retirement between his NHL and WHA playing years?
   A. One week
   B. One summer
   C. One year
   D. Two years

6.15 In what season will Wayne Gretzky reach the 3,000-point mark if he continues to play and score an average of 100 points per year?
   A. 1997–98
   B. 1998–99
   C. 1999–2000
   D. 2000–01

GORDIE & THE GREAT ONE
Answers

6.1   **D. 583 (Oilers) + 219 (Kings) = 802.**
Gretzky scored 583 goals—or 72.7% of 802 goals—with the Oilers before his move to Los Angeles where he netted another 219 goals (27.3%). Between October 14, 1979 and March 23, 1994, No. 99 scored 4 five-goal games, 9 four-goal games, 36 three-goal games, 141 two-goal games and 356 one-goal games.

6.2   **D. More than 2,400 games.**
Howe officially played in 2,421 NHL and WHA games, a total which does not include another estimated 300 exhibition matches, all-star appearances and international games in series against European teams. Howe's athletic durability is legendary. In his last season, he turned 52 years old and played the entire 80-game NHL schedule. In his 32-year career, Howe worked 18 complete seasons and missed only 103 regular season games out of a potential 2,186 matches.

6.3   **B. Kirk McLean.**
Gretzky shattered Howe's career goal-scoring record on March 23, 1994, potting his 802nd on a second-period, power-play goal against the Canucks' Kirk McLean. The Great One needed only 1,117 games to eclipse Howe's mark, which was set in 1,767 matches. Irbe was Gretzky's victim on goal No. 801 (March 20, 1994).

6.4   **C. The New England Whalers.**
Howe was a WHA Whaler when he became the first player in history to score 1,000 goals, beating John Garrett of the Birmingham Bulls on December 7, 1977. It was New England's first WHA season after moving from Houston where Howe as an Aero scored 141 goals in four years. Add his 853 goals as a Red Wing and

Howe was poised in 1977–78 to score his millennium history-maker. It could have happened in the NHL, but the league was outduelled by the Whalers, who signed the entire Howe family to long-term contracts.

6.5   A. Richard Brodeur.

Gretzky scored on 135 NHL goalies, but most often against the Canucks' Brodeur, who was victimized 29 times; more often than Liut (25), Greg Millen (21) and McLean (13). Even in the WHA, Brodeur couldn't escape the Gretzky jinx. While tending goal for the WHA Nordiques, Brodeur gave up two more Gretzky goals in No. 99's first pro season, 1978–79. The game dates: February 9 and March 7, 1979.

6.6   C. Playing alongside his sons, Mark and Marty.

Among the many milestones set by Gordie, his "biggest thrill" came in 1973 when he quit his Wings' retirement job, self-titled as the "vice-president in charge of paper clips," to play with Mark and Marty of the WHA Houston Aeros. One memorable story recalls a particular up-ice rush in 1978 when Mark, who normally used "Gordie" (or "Gramps") to address his father at the rink, impulsively yelled "Dad" for a quick pass. Gordie wired it on the tape and Mark fired a high shot into the top corner. It was one of hockey's special moments, audible to just a few players along the bench. In 1979, when the Whalers joined the NHL, so too did the Howes, becoming the league's first and only father-son combination to play together. Gordie was 51, Mark, 24.

6.7   B. Wiener.

Wayne's dad tried a couple of nicknames on him before one stuck. Walter Gretzky went from his son's given name, to "Wayner" and finally to "Wiener." The media christened him The Great One, but close friends simply call him Gretz.

6.8   D. It never happened.
Despite winning five Hart Trophies as league MVP, six
Art Ross Trophies as scoring champion and setting 11
NHL records, Howe never hit the magic 50-goal mark.
He came closest in 1952–53, scoring twice in the 68th
game for a total of 49 goals, one shy of tying arch-rival
Maurice Richard's 50-goal record. With two games left,
Howe was a lock, but Chicago held him scoreless and
Montreal threw everything at him, blanketing him
wherever he went on the ice so he would not beat the
Rocket's record. As Roy MacSkimming points out in
Gordie: A Hockey Legend, Howe was trying too hard, hitting goalposts, putting it over the net and on one glori-
ous opportunity "came painfully close to scoring number 50 when Lindsay, who had a chance to equal his
own career-high 33 goals, passed to him (Howe)
instead: 'The net was open,' Howe recalled, 'but before
Ted's pass got to me it nicked Hal Laycoe's skate and
skidded away.'" It was not to be. Howe had cleaned up
in the scoring race by an astounding margin of 24
points (34 ahead of the Richard), but he never got the
goal he really wanted.

6.9   D. More than 50 games.
Wayne Gretzky ripped off the NHL's longest and
hottest scoring streak by blasting 61 goals and 153
points in 51 consecutive games from October 5, 1983
through January 25, 1984. No. 99's record-setting point
run was finally halted on January 28th by the Kings'
Marcus Mattsson. Mario Lemieux holds the next
longest streak, scoring in 46 straight games (39–64–103)
in 1989–90.

6.10   C. Three times.
Despite their 33-year age difference, the hockey careers
of Howe and Gretzky did overlap two seasons, provid-
ing the opportunity for the pair to play opposite each
other on numerous occasions both in the WHA

(1978–79) and in the NHL (1979–80), but on only three occasions as teammates despite never being signed to the same franchise. That chance came at the 1979 WHA All-Star series, a three-game super-series between the WHA's best and the Moscow Dynamo. Coach Jacques Demers centred Wayne between Gordie and son Mark to produce the hottest line on the ice, scoring four goals that helped sweep the series. On one play Howe dug the puck out of the corner and feathered a pass to Gretzky in the slot. It was as if the old man of 50 had been playing all his career with the 17-year-old whiz kid. They also played in the NHL's 1980 All-Star contest, but on opposite sides—Howe on the Wales Conference roster defeated the Campbell Conference and Wayne Gretzky, 6–3. It was Howe's 23rd and final All-Star appearance and Gretzky's first as an NHLer.

6.11 A. 575.
The Great One wristed his 500th into an empty net on November 22, 1986 against Vancouver, Gretzky's 575th NHL game. A goals per game average of .869!

6.12 B. Most 20-or-more goal seasons.
Until Gretzky, Howe owned most of the league's career offensive records. He still holds a handful, including a record 22 (consecutive) 20-goal seasons when he was with Detroit between 1949 through 1971. Howe's record for most 30-goal seasons (14) was only broken in 1993–94 (by Mike Gartner), 24 years after Howe established it in 1970.

6.13 C. 40 to 50.
Gretzky had 46 empty net goals in his 802-goal career record. Among his most famous empty-netters are his career 100th and 500th goals, scored against Philadelphia on March 7, 1981 and Vancouver in 1986.

6.14   D. Two years.

Howe retired from the NHL in 1971 but played seven
more seasons beginning in 1973 when, at the age of 45,
he and sons Mark and Marty formed the all-Howe line
on the WHA's Houston Aeros. Despite his two-year
hiatus, Howe's natural hockey skills and athletic
resilience kept him competitive; maybe a stride slower,
he still played a physical, rock-solid finesse game, post-
ing personal best seasons of 96, 99, 100 and 102 points,
and winning two WHA championship Avco Cups. In
his last season, Howe returned to the NHL and scored
41 points, including a goal in his final game, against the
Canadiens' Denis Herron. It was Howe's *fifth* decade in
hockey.

6.15   C. 1999–2000.

All but one of Gretzky's 15 NHL seasons have been
plus 100-point years, so unless his back problems side-
line him again like in 1992–93 when he scored just 65
points, the Great One could be on course to score his
3,000th sometime in late 1999. Nineteen-*ninety-nine*.
Perfect. Wishful thinking or not, here's the math. In
1993–94, No. 99 scored 130 points, pushing him to
2,458. With enough ice time in 5½ seasons, he could easily score another 542 points.

THE GREAT ONE'S GREATEST POINT			
Season	Points	TP	Wayne's Age
1993-94	130	2458	33
1994-95	100	2558	34
1995-96	100	2658	35
1996-97	100	2758	36
1997-98	100	2858	37
1998-99	100	2958	38
1999	42	3000	38+

GAME 6

NUMBER CRUNCHING

In 1988's Stanley Cup Finals, Wayne Gretzky finally broke Gordie Howe's 33-year hold on the NHL record for most points in a final playoff series, by just one point. Gretzky scored 13 points on three goals and 10 assists in four games; and Howe, 12 points, five goals and seven assists in seven games in 1955's Cup final.

Here are some other numbers Mr. Hockey and No. 99 have made famous over the years. Match them with the clues provided below.

(Solutions are on page 118)

6	1988	215	2421	47	39
23	92	52	802	17	1971

1. _____ Gretzky's NHL record for fewest number of games to score 50 goals

2. _____ Howe's first jersey number with Detroit

3. _____ Wayne's league-record number of points in one playoff year

4. _____ Number of times Gordie won the NHL scoring race

5. _____ Wayne's record-breaking NHL career goal total

6. _____ Gordie's total number of games played in the NHL and WHA, regular and post season

7. _____ Year Gordie retired from Detroit

8. _____ Gretzky's league-leading season point total

9. _____ Howe's NHL-record for All-Star appearances

10. _____ Year Wayne got traded to Los Angeles

11. _____ Gordie's league record for age of eldest player to score an NHL goal

12. _____ Gretzky's NHL record for most season-goal total

7

THE RECORD-BREAKERS

Wayne Gretzky holds NHL records in most categories, including one that you won't find in any stat book or scoring sheet. The Great One leads all players in most trading cards produced from NHL-licensed card sets. Eleven different companies have issued a total of almost 300 cards with No. 99 on cardboard since 1979.

In this chapter, we boldly explore the murky depths of sports statistics by venturing into some of hockey's most offbeat records. While some are familiar, other records should push your envelope of trivia knowledge to the max.

(Answers are on page 76)

7.1 **What NHL record did Phil Esposito establish that Marcel Dionne tied, that Guy Lafleur soon broke, that later Mike Bossy set the standard of, but Wayne Gretzky could never top?**
A. Most 50-or-more goal seasons
B. Most three-or-more goal games, one season
C. Most goals one season by a centre
D. Most consecutive 50-or-more goal seasons

7.2 **Which expansion team holds the NHL record for most points in its first year?**
A. The Florida Panthers
B. The Philadelphia Flyers
C. The St. Louis Blues
D. The Anaheim Mighty Ducks

7.3 Since the 1967–68 expansion what is the fastest time a rookie has scored his first NHL goal in his first game (from the opening faceoff)?

A. Before the 20-second mark
B. Before the one-minute mark
C. Before the two-minute mark
D. Before the five-minute mark

7.4 What trio was the first NHL scoring line to finish 1–2–3 in the scoring race?

A. Montreal's Punch Line of Blake-Lach-Richard
B. Toronto's Kid Line of Jackson-Primeau-Conacher
C. Boston's Kraut Line of Dumart-Schmidt-Bauer
D. Detroit's Production Line of Lindsay-Abel-Howe

7.5 What NHL team holds the longest undefeated streak?

A. The Montreal Canadiens
B. The Detroit Red Wings
C. The Edmonton Oilers
D. The Philadelphia Flyers

7.6 Which junior holds the Western Hockey League record for most points in a season?

A. Cliff Ronning
B. Rob Brown
C. Ray Ferraro
D. Brian Propp

7.7 Who holds the Quebec Major Junior Hockey League record for most points in one season?

A. Guy Lafleur
B. Pat LaFontaine
C. Mario Lemieux
D. Pierre Larouche

7.8 Which Ontario Hockey League junior holds the OHL record for most points?
A. Bobby Smith
B. Jimmy Fox
C. Wayne Gretzky
D. Doug Gilmour

7.9 Who holds the all-time record for most goals in one season by a rookie in Canada's three junior leagues?
A. Pat LaFontaine
B. Tony Tanti
C. Wayne Gretzky
D. Don Murdoch

7.10 Who held the NHL's ironman mark before Garry Unger and Doug Jarvis?
A. Craig Ramsey
B. Alex Delvecchio
C. Andy Hebenton
D. Johnny "Iron Man" Wilson

7.11 What is the fastest time one player scored two goals in a playoff game?
A. Zero to five seconds
B. Six to 15 seconds
C. 16 to 30 seconds
D. More than 30 seconds

7.12 What NHL team record did Toronto set in 1934, that Buffalo tied in 1975, that neither Edmonton could break in the 1980s nor New Jersey or San Jose in the 1990s, but was only broken again by the Maple Leafs in 1993?
A. Longest winning streak
B. Longest winning streak from the start of the season
C. Longest winning streak including the playoffs
D. Longest undefeated streak in one season

7.13 Which club holds the NHL record for road victories by a first-year team?
A. The Florida Panthers
B. The Anaheim Mighty Ducks
C. The Tampa Bay Lightning
D. The San Jose Sharks

7.14 What is the NHL team record for most consecutive games without a goal?
A. Five games in a row
B. Six games in a row
C. Seven games in a row
D. Eight games in a row

7.15 Before Wayne Gretzky became the first NHLer to score 50 goals in fewer than 50 games, a WHA star did it. Who?
A. Quebec's Marc Tardif
B. Edmonton's Wayne Gretzky
C. Winnipeg's Anders Hedberg
D. Phoenix's Robbie Ftorek

7.16 Which NHL record did the Flyers' Tim Kerr set in 1985–86, that neither Dave Andreychuk, Joe Nieuwendyk, Mario Lemieux, Michel Goulet nor Brett Hull could break?
A. Most shorthanded goals in one season
B. Most goals in one period
C. Fastest two goals from the start of a period
D. Most power-play goals in one season

THE RECORD-BREAKERS
Answers

7.1 **D. Most consecutive 50-or-more goal seasons.**
This is one of Bossy's few NHL scoring records that was never broken by Gretzky, and never will now that the Great One is in his Californian sunset years.

MOST CONSECUTIVE 50-OR-MORE GOAL SEASONS			
Seasons	Player	Team	Years
9	M. Bossy	Islanders	'77-78/85-86
8	W. Gretzky	Oilers	'79-80/86-87
6	G. Lafleur	Canadiens	'74-75/79-80
5	M. Dionne	Kings	'78-79/82-83
5	P. Esposito	Bruins	'70-71/74-75

7.2 **A. The Florida Panthers.**
In 1993–94 the Panthers set an NHL expansion record, racking up 83 points in their inaugural season (84-game schedule) and recording the longest unbeaten streak (nine games) by a first-year team. But best remembered may be their tenacious season-long struggle for playoff

contention, only to fall short by one point after folding in the last two games. The Panthers had the league's third lowest goals against (233) but finished 22nd in scoring (233).

7.3   A. Before the 20-second mark.
It was a great start for a rookie in his season home opener. Just 18 seconds after the puck was dropped on October 10, 1974, Danny Gare, a 20-year old winger up from the Calgary Centennials, scored his first NHL goal on his first shift against the NHL's top scoring line, the Bruins' Phil Esposito, Wayne Cashman and Ken Hodge. What a night! Gare and the Sabres pounded the Bruins 9–5. Prior to expansion the fastest time is 15 seconds by Gus Bodnar (1943). More recently, Alexander Mogilny did it in 20 seconds (1989).

7.4   C. Boston's Kraut Line of Dumart-Schmidt-Bauer.
Milt Schmidt (52 points), Woody Dumart (43) and Bob Bauer (43) placed 1–2–3 in 1939–40, the first time three players from one club finished atop the NIIL's scoring race. The Kraut Line was one of hockey's most potent scoring threesomes, producing two Stanley Cups for Boston in 1939 and 1941. Honourable mention to Toronto's Kid Line, who came within a whisker of becoming the first team trio in 1931–32, but Howie Morenz finished one point ahead of fourth-place Charlie Conacher.

7.5   D. The Philadelphia Flyers
From October 14, 1979 through January 6, 1980 the Flyers amassed an undefeated streak that is unrivalled in pro hockey, winning 25 games and tying 10 in 35 straight matches. The string ended with a 7–1 loss to Minnesota, before the Flyers tore off on another 13-game undefeated streak. One measly loss in 49 games. Wow!

7.6   B. Rob Brown.

After being drafted in 1986 as Pittsburgh's fourth choice, 67th overall, Brown stayed another year in the WHL, set league records for most assists and points and won Canadian Major Junior Player of the Year in 1987. He was twice chosen WHL Player of the Year (1986, 1987).

THE WESTERN HOCKEY LEAGUE'S ALL-TIME TOP STARS						
Player	Season	Team	Games	G	A	TP
1 R. Brown	'86-87	Kamloops	72	76	136	212
2 C. Ronning	'84-85	New West.	70	89	108	197
3 B. Propp	'78-79	Brandon	71	94	100	194
4 R. Ferraro	'83-84	Brandon	72	108	84	192
5 J. Callander	'81-82	Regina	71	79	111	190
6 B. Federko	'75-76	Saskatoon	72	72	115	187
7 L. Barrie	'89-90	Kamloops	72	85	100	185

7.7   C. Mario Lemieux.

In his last junior year, 1983–84, Lemieux established himself as the next Quebec phenom, storming the QMJHL and averaging an astonishing four points per game (almost two goals a night) to dethrone Larouche, the long-reigning Quebecois record-holder, by an overwhelming 31-point spread. Judging by the volume of snipers clustered in our stat box (next page) from 1973–74, it was an offense-only season in Quebec junior hockey. Perhaps more indicative of great performance is the similar goal and game totals for Lemieux and Lafleur.

LA BELLE PROVINCE'S TOP SCORING JUNIOR STARS						
Player	Season	Team	Games	G	A	TP
1 M. Lemieux	'83-84	Laval	70	133	149	282
2 P. Larouche	'73-74	Sorel	67	94	157	251
3 P. LaFontaine	'82-83	Verdun	70	104	130	234
4 M. Deziel	'73-74	Sorel	69	92	135	227
5 R. Cloutier	'73-74	Quebec	69	93	123	216
6 J. Cossette	'73-74	Sorel	68	97	117	214
7 G. Lafleur	'70-71	Quebec	62	130	79	209

7.8 A. Bobby Smith.

Smith's record junior season in 1977-78 made him Minnesota's overwhelming choice for first overall in the 1978 NHL draft. He not only burned up Ontario's record books in scoring but was named to centre position on the OHL's first All-Star team and voted Canadian Major Junior Player of the Year, both in 1978. In his first NHL season, Smith scored 74 points and won Calder Trophy as rookie of the year.

THE ONTARIO HOCKEY LEAGUE'S ALL-TIME TOP STARS						
Player	Season	Team	Games	G	A	TP
1 B. Smith	'77-78	Ottawa	61	69	123	192
2 W. Gretzky	'77-78	SS/Marie	64	70	112	182
3 D. Gilmour	'82-83	Cornwall	68	70	107	177
4 M. Kaszychi	'75-76	SS/Marie	66	50	119	170
5 J. Fox	'79-80	Ottawa	52	65	101	166
6 J. Goodwin	'80-81	SS/Marie	68	58	110	166
7 B. Boudreau	'74-75	Toronto	69	68	97	165

7.9   A. Pat LaFontaine.
American-born LaFontaine cut a wide swath through
the Quebec Major Junior Hockey League in his rookie
year, 1982–83, scoring 104 goals in 70 games with the
Verdun Jr. Canadiens. LaFontaine, a St. Louis, Missouri
native who learned hockey in Detroit before playing
junior in Montreal, has scored more goals than any
other rookie in Canadian junior hockey history. Next
best are: Murdoch with 82 goals for Medicine Hat
(WHL) in 1974–75; Tanti with 81 goals, Oshawa (OHL),
1980–81; and Gretzky with 70 goals, Sault St. Marie
(OHL), 1977–78.

7.10   C. Andy Hebenton.
Winnipeg-born Hebenton played 630 games in nine
complete 70-game seasons, never missing a contest in
his entire NHL career with New York and Boston from
1955 through 1964. In 1976, Hebenton's record was broken by Unger whose own mark was outrun by Jarvis on
December 26, 1986. Ramsey played 776 games but did-
n't break any records since Unger stayed ahead of him
in consecutive games; Delvecchio hit 490 and, in one
stretch of his remarkable 24-year career with Detroit,
sat out just 12 games in 1,158 matches.

	THE NHL'S HEAVY METTLE MARATHON MEN (The Record-Breakers)[*]			
Games	Player	Team	Complete Seasons	Years
508	Murray Murdoch	New York	11	1926–37
580	Johnny Wilson	Det-Chi-Tor	8+	1952–60
630	Andy Hebenton	NYR-Bos	9	1955–64
914	Garry Unger	Tor-Det/ St.L-Atl	11+	1968–79
964	Doug Jarvis	Mtl-Hfd-Wsh	12	1975–87

[*] *In chronological order*

7.11 A. Zero to five seconds.

On April 11, 1965 Detroit's Norm Ullman set a playoff record for the fastest two goals—five seconds. Ullman scored on Glenn Hall at 17:35 and 17:40 of the second period, giving the Red Wings the lead and adding another in the third for a hat trick and a Red Wing 4–2 win over Chicago.

7.12 B. Longest winning streak from the start of the season.

In 1993 the Maple Leafs bolted from the NHL blocks and won their first 10 season starts, breaking the old NHL record of eight straight victories that they set 61 years earlier and which was tied by Buffalo in 1975. The 10-win streak—against Chicago (twice), Dallas, Detroit (twice), Hartford, Washington, Philadelphia, Tampa Bay and Florida—ended after a 5–2 loss to coach Pat Burns's former team, the Canadiens, on October 30, 1993. Ex-Leaf Vincent Damphousse scored a hat trick and Patrick Roy recorded the win over Felix Potvin, who had a brilliant 1.89 GAA in the ten starts, outsaving the opposition by a combined score of 45-20.

LONGEST WINNING STREAK FROM SEASON START

Consecutive #/Wins	Team	Year
10	Toronto Maple Leafs	1993–94
8	Toronto Maple Leafs	1934–35
8	Buffalo Sabres	1975–76
7	Edmonton Oilers	1983–84
7	Quebec Nordiques	1985–86
7	Pittsburgh Penguins	1986–87
7	New Jersey Devils	1993–94

Current to 1993–94

7.13 B. The Anaheim Mighty Ducks.
Their half-million-dollar Disney-produced home-opening extravaganza aside, the Ducks saved their best show for the road with a 19–20–3 record, a respectable 13th among the NHL's 26 teams. It was the best away record ever for a first-year expansion team and just ahead of the Panthers who posted 18–16–8 the same season, 1993-94. At home the Ducks were 14–26–2 in their first year or 25th overall in the home-wins column.

7.14 D. Eight games in a row.
The Chicago Blackhawks went scoreless for an unprecedented eight straight games in 1928–29, losing or tying 1–0, 1–0, 1–0, 3–0, 3–0, 0–0, 3–0 and 0–0 in almost a month of action. The shutout streak began February 7th in New York against the Americans and ending mercifully March 2 with a 2–1 win over the Montreal Maroons. Chicago, in just its third NHL season and easily the league's worst team, was goose-egged another 12 times. The 'Hawks won only seven matches in the 44-game schedule.

7.15 C. Winnipeg's Anders Hedberg.
The first player in professional hockey to break one of the game's most prestigious records, 50-in-50, was Hedberg, who smashed Maurice Richard's mark set in 1945 by scoring 51 goals in 49 Jets games (his 47th match) in 1976–77. Playing with a cracked rib that had already sidelined him for two games and was supposed to put him out indefinitely, the Jets' Swedish winger popped eight goals in games 47 and 48, and then on February 6, 1977 against the Calgary Cowboys (game 49) he scored goals 49, 50 and 51, finally surpassing the Rocket's milestone.

7.16 D. Most power-play goals in one season.

In 1985–86 Tim Kerr scored an NHL record 34 power-play goals with Philadelphia, almost equalled by Andreychuk (32) and Hull (29) twice, in 1990–91 and 1992–93.

	NHL POWER-MEN ON POWER-PLAY GOALS		
Goals	**Player**	**Team**	**Year**
34	T. Kerr	Flyers	1985-86
32	D. Andreychuk	Sabres/Leafs	1992-93
31	J. Nieuwendyk	Flames	1987-88
31	M. Lemieux	Penguins	1988-89
29	M. Goulet	Nordiques	1987-88
29	B. Hull	Blues	1990-91 & 1992-93

Current to 1993-94

Across

1. Faultfinder, an armchair _____
5. A goalie _____ the shot
8. Home town of the Kings
9. Negotiations
11. Exchange players
13. Offensive area at net
14. _____ a good prospect
15. _____-_____ it
17. Time _____
19. A clean _____
23. Canadian sports TV network
25. Offensive style of play, begun by Habs and used by Oilers (3 words)
28. Puck took a _____ hop
29. Centre of ice
31. Jerry _____
33. Best of _____
34. Player was _____ into the boards
37. _____ home
39. Dressing room _____
41. _____ income
42. Islander who scored 1st Cup winner, Bob _____
44. Boston GM
48. Central Red _____ team
49. _____ MacInnis
50. "_____ what you will."
51. A pass to your opponent
54. Oldtimer
56. Sniper
58. Red Wing, Norm _____
61. Ex-Penguin, Bob _____
63. Brian Leetch's country, abbrev.
64. Gets really mad, goes _____
65. _____ Howe
66. Overtime, abbrev.
67. Illegal use of stick
68. _____ are the champions.

Down

1. Let go from team
2. ____-tempered
3. Push your opponent against the dasher (4 words)
4. Letters on Canadiens' crest
6. ____ a goal in by mistake
7. Cup winners
10. _____ Division
12. "_____ up time"
16. 1980s journeyman, Gary _____
18. _____ on two
19. _____ Stove League
20. _____ the slot
21. Sylvain Cote's uniform no.
22. Block view
23. _____ Lindsay
24. ____Apps
26. _____ the bench
27. _____ Daneyko
30. Kind of goalie stop (2 words)
31. Hartford winger Robert _____
32. 1940s goalie, _____ Grant
35. Canadiens coach
36. _____ Tikkanen
37. Upper limb
38. Trifle or _____ with your opponent
40. Wayne's old team
43. A Los Angeles shake
45. An empty-net goal is _____
46. Where MSG is, abbrev.
47. Best defenseman ever
52. _____ the defense
53. 1960s journeyman, Duane _____
55. Attempt
57. Injured, _____ of action
59. _____ Fogolin
60. _____ Jersey
62. _____ Belfour
64. "_____ usual"

THE CROSSWORD

(Solution is on page 118)

8

THE SUPERSTARS

There's little doubt that scoring goals and skilful playmaking are the big reasons why legions of hockey fans return to the game each season. Low-scoring contests can be thrilling to watch, especially those cliffhangers backstopped by exceptional goaltending. But nothing compares to the free-wheeling action of a coast-to-coast rush, bang-bang plays in the attacking zone or 100 mph slappers that bulge the net and send a crowd into pandemonium.

Hockey is a split-second sport. Games are won and lost, and championships decided, on the reflexes, mobility and perception of players, who in an instant can shift a game's momentum with a big hit, a crucial save or goal. Those who do it with consistency are hockey's superstars.

(Answers are on page 89)

8.1 Who was the first NHLer to have his jersey retired?
A. The Canadiens' Howie Morenz
B. The Bruins' Lionel Hitchman
C. The Maple Leafs' Ace Bailey
D. The Canadiens' Maurice Richard

8.2 Who scored the fastest 100 goals (from the start of a career) in NHL history?
A. Brett Hull
B. Wayne Gretzky
C. Mike Bossy
D. Teemu Selanne

8.3 Who was the first NHLer to score *more than* 50 goals in a season?
A. Maurice Richard
B. Bobby Hull
C. Bernie Geoffrion
D. Phil Esposito

8.4 Who is the only player inducted into the Hall of Fame after being banished from NHL play?
A. Babe Pratt
B. Billy Smith
C. Eddie Shore
D. Ted Lindsay

8.5 Name the only two players in NHL history to top 50 goals, 100 points and 200 penalty minutes in one season?
A. Bobby Clarke and Dino Ciccarelli
B. Mark Messier and Theoren Fleury
C. Jeremy Roenick and Cam Neely
D. Kevin Stevens and Brendan Shanahan

8.6 Who is the first Russian in the NHL to win the Hart Trophy as league MVP?
A. Sergei Makarov
B. Pavel Bure
C. Sergei Fedorov
D. Alexander Mogilny

8.7 Who was the first NHLer to score 50 goals in 50 games after Maurice Richard first set the record in 1945?
A. Bernie Geoffrion
B. Bobby Hull
C. Phil Esposito
D. Mike Bossy

8.8 **Which superstar didn't score in his first NHL game?**
A. Gordie Howe
B. Eric Lindros
C. Wayne Gretzky
D. Mario Lemieux

8.9 **How many empty-net goals has Brett Hull scored in his first 500 regular-season games?**
A. Only one
B. Between one and ten
C. Between ten and 20
D. More than 20

8.10 **Which NHL scoring leader has the most penalty minutes of any Art Ross Trophy winner in league history?**
A. Stan Mikita
B. Ted Lindsay
C. Gordie Howe
D. Bryan Trottier

8.11 **Who is the youngest NHLer to score 100 points?**
A. Wayne Gretzky
B. Dale Hawerchuk
C. Mario Lemieux
D. Jimmy Carson

8.12 **Besides Gordie Howe, who is the only other player to score 1,000 goals in professional hockey?**
A. Phil Esposito
B. Bobby Hull
C. Wayne Gretzky
D. Mike Gartner

8.13 Who was the first Russian to record a 50-goal season?
A. Alexander Mogilny
B. Sergei Fedorov
C. Alexei Kovalev
D. Pavel Bure

8.14 What personal record did Mike Gartner accomplish in 1991–92?
A. His 500th goal
B. His 500th assist
C. His 1,000th point
D. His 1,000th game

8.15 Name the only brother combination to make the first All-Star team in the same year and do it twice.
A. Maurice and Henri Richard
B. Frank and Pete Mahovlich
C. Charlie and Lionel Conacher
D. Phil and Tony Esposito

THE SUPERSTARS
Answers

8.1 C. The Maple Leafs' Ace Bailey
Bailey is probably the very first athlete to have his player number retired in North American professional sports, certainly in hockey, when on February 14, 1934, the Toronto Maple Leafs honoured their scoring champ by staging the NHL's inaugural benefit All-Star game and retiring his sweater, No. 6. The tribute came just months after Bailey sustained a severe skull fracture in

an sickening on-ice collision that left him near death except for two delicate brain operations. His forced retirement from hockey marked the first time the league's best players met in an all-star contest. No pro sports figure had previously been so honoured. The Canadiens retired Morenz's No. 7 in 1937, the Yankees, Lou Gehrig's No. 4 in 1939 and the New York Giants, Ray Flaherty's No. 1 in 1935. Bailey was the first Maple Leaf ever to win the NHL scoring race.

8.2   C. Mike Bossy.
After demolishing Bossy's rookie-record of 53 goals in 1992–93 by an incredible 23-goal margin, Selanne (76 goals) was poised, in 1993–94, to become the NHL's fastest 100-goal scorer. But the sophomore jinx played havoc with the Finnish sniper whose 23 goals in 44 games left him one short of tying Bossy's 100-goal mark in 129 games. Selanne scored No. 100 a game late, his 130th NHL match, on January 12, 1994 in a 3–2 win over Buffalo.

8.3   B. Bobby Hull.
After Richard scored 50 goals in the 50-game 1945 schedule, 21 years passed before Bobby Hull topped him on March 12, 1966, gunning No. 51 beyond Ranger goalie Cesare Maniago.

8.4   A. Babe Pratt.
Pratt, a 1940s Bobby Orr-type of rushing defenseman with the scoring points and Hart Trophy to prove it, received a "lifetime banishment" from NHL president Red Dutton after admitting he had gambled on Maple Leaf games. Upon review and a plea for mercy by Pratt, the league's board of governors voted the all-star rear-guard back into the NHL only weeks after the scandal broke. Pratt played his best years with Toronto and was inducted into the Hall of Fame in 1966.

8.5   D. Kevin Stevens and Brendan Shanahan.

When Stevens racked up totals of 54 goals, 123 points and 254 penalty minutes in 1991-92, the Penguins' winger became the first NHLer to combine soft hands and hard knocks into a league record—the 50–100–200 masterpiece. His *tour de force* was matched in 1993–94 by Blues forward Shanahan, who became known in St. Louis as "Shan the Man," a nickname harking back to the baseball Cardinals' legendary Stan "The Man" Musial. Both play(ed) their respective sports with power and finesse: Musial hit a torrid .702 (slugging average) for St. Louis in 1948 (the last player to slug above .700 in the NL); and Shanahan potted 52 goals and 102 points while collecting 211 penalty minutes.

8.6   C. Sergei Fedorov.

Whether wearing the red of his former Central Red Army team or his present-day Red Wings, Fedorov has always displayed the true colours of his phenomenal talent, winning two World Championships in 1989 and 1990 and, in 1994, two NHL awards as top defensive forward (Frank Selke Trophy) and league MVP (Hart Trophy), after scoring 56 goals and 120 points. Any player who can accomplish that and make superstar Steve Yzerman almost dispensable to a team deserves to be an MVP.

8.7   D. Mike Bossy.

Hockey's most famous record had been safe for 35 years; more than 12,000 NHL games played by the likes of Bobb Hull, Phil Esposito and Guy Lafleur, all failing to equal the Rocket's 50-in-50 mark. Until Bossy, who predicted at the start of 1980–81 that he would be the next one. That arched a few eyebrows around the league. Yes, he had three remarkable plus 50-goal seasons during his meteoric ascent to superstar status as the triggerman of the NHL's hottest line, the Islanders'

Grande Trio with Bryan Trottier and Clark Gillies. But 50-in-50? Sure enough, Bossy's prediction was in big trouble late in game 50 on January 24, 1981. Stalled at 48 goals with only four minutes remaining, that's when the Boss Man took over. In a mad goal-mouth scramble he backhanded goal 49 and, then, with just 89 seconds left, goal 50 went in, matching the Rocket's record. Afterwards, Bossy graciously acknowledged his accomplishment, joking that Richard still held the record because the Rocket's 50th came faster—with 2:15 remaining on the clock.

8.8   C. Wayne Gretzky.

The Great One didn't score his first NHL goal until his fifth game (October 14, 1979), a backhanded fan shot which dribbled through the legs of Vancouver's Glen Hanlon. Howe, wearing No. 17, scored (on Turk Broda) in his first NHL game on October 16, 1946; as did Lemieux (first game, first shift, first shot on Pete Peeters) on October 11, 1984; and Lindros (Tom Barrasso) on October 6, 1992.

8.9   A. Only one.

Hull's first empty-net goal didn't come until his 500th regular season game, a mixed milestone considering his dislike of empty-netters which he believes cheapens a goal scorer's record. (Contrarily, Hull seldom sees too many empty nets since, as a defensive liability, he isn't on the ice to protect one-goal leads.) However, on January 13, 1994, with his Blues ahead by just a goal and no one to pass the puck off to, Hull reluctantly slid his first into an Oilers' open net. It was the Golden Brett's 386th goal.

8.10   A. Stan Mikita.

Mikita set the standard for box time among all NHL scoring leaders, twice racking up more PIM than any other Art Ross winner: 146 penalty minutes in 1963-64 and 154 in 1964–65. Notorious for his chippy attitude, with opponent and official alike, Mikita overcame his retaliatory streak to win two consecutive Lady Byng Trophies for sportsmanship and gentlemanly conduct in 1966–67 (12 PIM) and 1967–68 (14 PIM), the same years he was awarded Art Ross Trophies as scoring leader and Hart Trophies as league MVP. In recent times, Mario Lemieux recorded one of the NHL's highest penalty minute totals for a scoring leader, 100 PIM in 1988–89.

THE NHL'S MOST PENALIZED SCORING LEADERS

Player	Team	Season	TP	PIM
S. Mikita	Chicago	1964–65	87	154
S. Mikita	Chicago	1963–64	89	146
J. Beliveau	Montreal	1955–56	88	143
T. Lindsay	Detroit	1949–50	78	141
B. Orr	Boston	1969–70	120	125
N. Stewart	Maroons	1925–26	42	119

Current to 1993–94

8.11 B. Dale Hawerchuk.

Hawerchuk fulfilled all of the Jets' expectations as 1981's first overall draft pick, winning the Calder Trophy as top rookie and breaking the 100-point barrier at 18 years, 11 months old. Hawerchuk, who became the NHL's youngest 100-point man on March 24, 1982, beat Gretzky in age by three months.

8.12 B. Bobby Hull.

The only other player who can claim a career goal total in excess of 1,000 goals is Hull, who scored his 1,000th three months after Howe. Both were playing in the WHA, Howe with New England and Hull as a Jet, when, on March 11, 1978, he notched No. 1,000 against the Quebec Nordiques.

HOCKEY'S TWO MILLENNIUM MEN				
	Gordie Howe		Bobby Hull	
	RS	Playoff	RS	Playoff
NHL	801	68	610	62
WHA	174	28	303	43
Total Goals	1,071		1,018	

8.13 A. Alexander Mogilny.

Mogilny became the NHL's first Russian 50-goal scorer on February 3, 1993, 26 days earlier than Bure, who popped his 50th on March 1, 1993. Mogilny scored No. 50 in his 46th game of 1992–93, beating Hartford's Sean Burke with only 28 seconds remaining in regulation time for the 3–2 win. He was 23 years old.

8.14 A. B. C. D. His 500th goal & assist and 1,000th point & game.

Okay, so we didn't provide an "All of the above" answer among our multiple choices, but Gartner did set four individual records in 1991–92, the first NHLer to register his 500th goal, 500th assist, 1,000th point and 1,000th game all in same season.

8.15 D. Phil and Tony Esposito.

The Espositos are the only brothers twice voted to the first All-Star team in two different years, 1970 and 1972. The only other brothers to both be selected to the first All-Star team in the same year are the Conachers in 1934. Neither the Richards nor the Mahovliches ever succeeded in peaking at the same time.

GAME 8

THE 500-GOAL CLUB

Membership in the 500-goal club is very exclusive. Only 20 players in NHL history have the credentials to join this Who's Who of hockey. The founding member was Maurice Richard in 1957; sometime in 1994–95 (or when he's back to strength) Mario Lemieux will pot his 500th and become the twentieth and newest associate in this class unto itself. Find the famous 20 who have scored 500 goals reading across, down or diagonally. Like our example of Gilbert P-E-R-R-E-A-U-L-T, connect the name using letters no more than once and start at the letters printed in heavy type.

(Solution is on page 118)

9

SHOOTOUTS

When Olympic gold was decided in a heart-stopping shootout between then-future NHL stars Peter Forsberg and Paul Kariya at the 1994 Winter Games, it became obvious that international hockey had a bona fide crowd-pleaser for deciding tie games, one the NHL could no longer ignore. Should the league's greatest snipers duel one-on-one with goaltenders for the game-winner? Or is a tie still an outcome, only to be determined by the entire team in overtime? In this true or false quiz, take the long solo rush in from centre ice and test your shooting strength on new facts and also your stick-handling abilities around some trivia covered in previous chapters. Score the shootout winner and make the playoffs in the next chapter.

(Answers are on page 99)

9.1 **The crossbar, not a player's shoulder, is the determining factor for high-stick goals.**
True or False?

9.2 **Wayne Gretzky scored his very first professional goal against the Edmonton Oilers.** True or False?

9.3 **Pavel Bure is the NHL's highest drafted Russian.**
True or False?

9.4 **The Florida Panthers are the first NHL team to regularly broadcast games in Spanish.**
True or False?

9.5 No defenseman in NHL history has ever registered a five-goal game. True or False?

9.6 Neil Broten was the only American from the 1980 Olympic Dream Team still playing in the NHL in 1993–94. True or False?

9.7 Wendel Clark is the first Maple Leaf captain ever traded directly to a Quebec-based NHL team. True or False?

9.8 There is no centre red line in professional roller hockey. True or False?

9.9 The very first player in NHL history awarded a penalty shot failed to score. True or False?

9.10 The *American* Hockey League has teams on both sides of the U.S.-Canada border, while the *International* Hockey League is based only in the United States. True or False?

9.11 Gordie Howe scored in his first NHL game. True or False?

9.12 The 1993–94 Los Angeles Kings are the first team, since the 1967 expansion, to miss the playoffs one year after playing in a Cup final. True or False?

9.13 Goalies are more successful at stopping shooters in penalty shot situations during the playoffs than the regular season. True or False?

9.14 Wayne Gretzky was runner-up to Mike Gartner as WHA Rookie of the Year in 1979. True or False?

9.15 No brother combination from the same team has ever made the first All-Star team in the same **year.** True or False?

9.16 Jari Kurri was the first European-trained player to score 1,000 points in the NHL. True or False?

9.17 Red Kelly scored more goals on defense with Detroit than as a centre with Toronto.
True or False?

9.18 Guy Lafleur was the last player from an "Original Six" team to win the Art Ross Trophy as the NHL's leading scorer. True or False?

9.19 Gordie Howe never wore a helmet. True or False?

9.20 Only once have two players been chosen to the same position on the first All-Star team.
True or False?

9.21 Both the 1994 World Championship and Olympic gold medals were decided by shootouts.
True or False?

9.22 Only one penalty shot has ever been awarded in overtime in playoff action. True or False?

SHOOTOUTS
Answers

9.1 True.

In Section six, Rule 58 (B) of the NHL's official rules, it states that a goal scored by an attacking player who strikes the puck with his stick above the height of the crossbar shall not be allowed. But, if a defending player scores a goal in his own net while his stick is above the height of the crossbar, that counts.

9.2 True.

Just 17 years old and a rookie centre with the World Hockey Association's Indianapolis Racers, Gretzky scored his first pro goal against Dave Dryden and the WHA Oilers on October 20, 1978. It was Gretzky's fourth game in the big leagues.

9.3 False.

Bure was chosen 113th overall in 1989. Yashin (Ottawa, 2nd overall/1992) and Oleg Tverdovsky (Florida, 2nd overall/1994) are the highest-drafted Russians, followed by Darius Kasparaitis (Islanders, 5th overall 1992) and Viktor Kozlov (San Jose, 6th overall 1993).

9.4 True.

When radio play-by-play announcer Arley Londono called the Panthers' first game on October 6, 1993, it established an NHL first: the inaugural Spanish broadcast of a hockey game. Since most Florida Hispanics had never even seen hockey played much less understood calls like icing or high sticking, Londono described it as a sport with the rules of soccer, the aggressiveness of American football—and a little like boxing.

9.5   False.

The NHL's only blueliner to notch five goals in a single game is Toronto's Ian Turnbull, who riddled Detroit netminders Ed Giacomin and Jim Rutherford in a 9–1 win in 1977.

9.6   False.

Broten, named All-American at the University of Minnesota in 1981 and gold medalist in hockey at the 1980 Olympics, is playing his 14th season (1994–95) with the Stars, but he was not the only NHLer active in 1993–94 that played for America's famed Dream Team. Defenseman Mike Ramsey (Pittsburgh) and winger Dave Christian (Chicago) were also in Lake Placid when Team USA battled the feared Soviet Red Machine and the Finnish National Team to win gold. Broten, Ramsey and Christian are all from Minnesota.

9.7   True.

When GM Cliff Fletcher did the unspeakable and traded away the Leafs' heart and soul to the Nordiques in 1994, Clark became not only the first Toronto captain traded to a Quebec team, but just the second Leaf C in the club's 68-year history ever to play with Montreal or Quebec. Rob Ramage, who captained the Leafs from 1989 to 1991, skated briefly with the Habs in 1993 after stints with Minnesota and Tampa Bay. The Clark deal gave Fletcher some nice offensive spark (Mats Sundin) to centre the second line, and Quebec finally got a team leader who will give 110% every game.

9.8   False.

In Roller Hockey International, there is a centre red line, but the bluelines have been eliminated, which means fewer offsides, more action and more offense.

9.9 True.

Three games into 1934–35, the first season the penalty shot rule was in force, Armand Mondou of the Montreal Canadiens was awarded the NHL's first penalty shot. But the night belonged to Leaf goalie George Hainsworth, who stopped Mondou and became the first goalie to prevent a penalty shot goal. It happened on November 10, 1934. The Leafs won 2–1 in overtime.

9.10 True.

The names of minor hockey's two top leagues contradict their true geographic representation: the AHL has an international contingent of teams and the IHL is not represented beyond the American borders (although "I" teams did play against CSKA Moscow for points in the 1993–94 standings and could go to Europe under expansion plans in 1995–96).

9.11 True.

Howe netted No. 1 of 801 NHL goals in his first game on October 16, 1946. Howe's first victim was Toronto goalie Turk Broda.

9.12 False.

After winning the Cup in 1969, the Montreal Canadiens failed to make the playoffs in 1970, despite amassing 92 points in 76 games; high numbers in any season, especially when compared to the 1994 Kings, who dropped to just 66 points in 84 games—five points less than the first-year Mighty Ducks.

9.13 True.

During the regular season goalies have a 55.8% success rate to shooters 44.2%, but come playoff time that rate skyrockets to 64.3% in favour of netminders, who in 28 penalty shot attempts in playoff history have blanked shooters 18 times.

9.14 False.
In fact, Gartner, who played his rookie season in Cincinnati with the WHA Stingers, was Gretzky's runner-up as WHA Rookie of the Year in 1979. In the WHA scoring race, Gretzky finished third (behind Real Cloutier and Robbie Ftorek) with a 46–64–110 record, while Gartner managed 27–25–52. It's the only time in his lengthy career that Gartner, the NHL's record holder of most consecutive 30-or-more goal seasons (15), didn't score 30 goals.

9.15 True.
Only the Espositos in 1970 and 1972 and Conachers in 1934 have ever been selected to the first All-Star team in the same year, but neither brother combination was from the same team; Phil played for Boston and Tony for Chicago, while Lionel was with Chicago and Charlie with Toronto.

9.16 False.
Peter Stastny of the Quebec Nordiques was the first European to record 1,000 career points. The Czech defector did it on October 19, 1989, two months and 14 days before Kurri's 1,000th, January 2, 1990.

9.17 True.
Before Kelly was traded to the Maple Leafs, where he scored 119 goals as a centre in 7½ seasons, he spent 12½ years on Detroit's blueline, recording 162 goals, the most among all defensemen of his era.

9.18 True.
The last time an "Original Six" player won the NHL scoring race was in 1978 when Guy Lafleur scored 132 points. Since then, Wayne Gretzky (Edmonton, Los Angeles) and Mario Lemieux (Pittsburgh) have monopolized the Art Ross Trophy an unprecedented 14 times

between them and only two other players, Bryan Trottier (the Islanders) in 1979 and Marcel Dionne (Los Angeles) in 1980, have won it.

9.19 False.

In 32 years, Howe wore a helmet only once, in 1950–51. After sustaining a severe concussion in a dangerous collision with Toronto's Ted Kennedy late in 1949–50, Howe came back the following season donning a leather helmet. As was once the custom, players only used helmets after a serious injury.

9.20 True.

The only time in NHL All-Star history that two NHLers were named to the same player position on the first team was in 1938 when Gord Drillon of Toronto shared right wing honours with the Rangers' Cecil Dillon. As a result of the tie in balloting, both were officially named right wingers to the first and second All-Star teams.

9.21 True.

Sweden's Peter Forsberg and Canada's Luc Robitaille scored the sudden-death shootout winners that won gold medals for their respective countries at the 1994 Olympics and World Championships.

9.22 False.

In playoff history, 28 penalty shots have been called, but never once during an overtime.

"FOR TEE-OFF TIME INFO, CALL 1-800-U-BLEW-IT"

The 1994 playoffs produced a wide assortment of ingenious spectator signboards. And long overdue, too. After an uninspired regular season of little placard artwork, hockey fans finally got it together in post-season and drew up the most clever passages this side of the graffiti wall. For example, "For Tee-Off Time Info, Call 1-800-U-Blew-It" was one of the better signboard snubs aimed at team rivals of (who else?) New York Ranger fans. Nothing like a little welcoming shot-in-the-arm at MSG.

Special credit to those four barrel-chested Shark fans (with the soft underbellies), who each painted their naked upper torsos with a large black letter, together spelling I-R-B-E, the name of their Latvian star goalie. Really ugly, but good work, fellas. You win this year's honours for best Spectator Sign in a Living Body category.

In this game, the challenge is to match the hometown arenas with the appropriate slogans taken from real spectator signboards. Each slogan heralds a specific hockey event in 1993–94, either from regular season or playoff action.

(Solutions are on page 119)

Chicago Stadium	Buffalo's Memorial Auditorium
Hartford Civic Center	New Jersey's Meadowlands Arena
Dallas's Reunion Arena	Nassau Veterans' Memorial Coliseum
Montreal Forum	Detroit's Joe Louis Arena
Ottawa Civic Centre	Vancouver's Pacific Coliseum
The Pond of Anaheim	Toronto's Maple Leaf Gardens
San Jose Arena	Washington's U.S. Air Arena

1. _____ "Doesn't Matter What Kind Of Fish: Cod, Tuna, Shark. They All Stink."

2. _____ "We Got The Bowl. We Want The Cup."

3. _____ "Vive Les Champions."

4. _____ "What Do We Need The Big Apple For, When We've Got Cherry."

5. _____ "Is It Live Or Is It Messmerex?"

6. _____ "Never Say Dielanders."

7. _____ "Way To Go Dino, 500 Goals."

8. _____ "Bring Back Brad."

9. _____ "Quack Attack."

10. _____ "Welcome Back Dale, We Missed You."

11. _____ "And The Shark Devoureth The Octopus. John 94:16."

12. _____ "Alexander The Great."

13. _____ "At Least We Ain't Last."

14. _____ "Devil Fans: Quality Not Quantity."

10

THE MIRACLE ON 33RD STREET
(AND OTHER TRUE STORIES)

After suffering through more than five Cup-less decades and countless unending chants of "1940, 1940," the New York Rangers and their fans finally put the Stanley Cup curse to rest in 1994 by narrowly defeating the pesky Canucks 3-2 in game seven. It was a storybook championship season for the NHL, flush full of Cinderella teams, come-from-behind thrillers, Russian superstars and MVP performances that were crowned or crushed by huge goals and saves. It was not unlike other playoff seasons, except now all can hail the champions: "1994, 1994."

(Answers are on page 110)

10.1 **In which 1994 playoff round and before which game did Ranger captain Mark Messier make his "Babe Ruth" prediction about winning the next game?**
A. Conference semifinals—Game six against the Capitals
B. Conference finals—Game six against the Devils
C. Cup finals—Game six against the Canucks
D. Cup finals—Game seven against the Canucks

10.2 Which defenseman holds the record for most points in one playoff year?
A. Paul Coffey
B. Al MacInnis
C. Denis Potvin
D. Brian Leetch

10.3 Who was the oldest goalie ever to appear in a playoff game?
A. Jacques Plante
B. Lester Patrick
C. Johnny Bower
D. Glenn Hall

10.4 Who was the first NHLer to score on a penalty shot in a playoff game?
A. Jim Roberts
B. Wayne Connelly
C. Frank Mahovlich
D. Bill Barber

10.5 What tunnel was used to travel from New York City to New Jersey in the "Tunnel Series" between the Devils and the Rangers in 1994's Stanley Cup semi-final series?
A. The Holland Tunnel
B. The Washington Tunnel
C. The Lincoln Tunnel
D. The Memorial Tunnel

10.6 How many times, if any, in NHL history has a sub-.500 regular season team gone on to win the Stanley Cup?
A. Only once
B. Two times
C. Four times
D. It has never happened,

10.7 Who was the youngest player in the 1994 playoffs?
A. San Jose's Vlastimil Kroupa
B. Vancouver's Nathan LaFayette
C. Boston's Bryan Smolinski
D. New Jersey's Jim Dowd

10.8 Which Ranger is the only NHLer to score a sudden-death goal in two multiple-overtime games in the same playoff series?
A. Brian Leetch
B. Stephane Matteau
C. Alexei Kovalev
D. Mark Messier

10.9 Which NHL franchise had the most American-born talent on its Stanley Cup-winning team?
A. The New York Islanders
B. The Chicago Blackhawks
C. The Detroit Red Wings
D. The Pittsburgh Penguins

10.10 Among these four Conn Smythe winners, which player is different from the other three based on their playoff performances against the Montreal Canadiens?
A. Roger Crozier
B. Glenn Hall
C. Reggie Leach
D. Ron Hextall

10.11 How many times, if any, in seven attempts have players scored on penalty shots awarded in the Stanley Cup finals?
A. Only once
B. Three times
C. Four times
D. It has never happened.

10.12 How much did the NHL pay each member of the New York Rangers for winning the Stanley Cup in 1940?
A. Between $500 and $1,000
B. Between $1,000 and $1,500
C. Between $1,500 and $3,000
D. More than $3,000

10.13 Who was the last maskless goalie to win a Stanley Cup?
A. The Canadiens' Gump Worsley
B. The Maple Leafs' Johnny Bower
C. The Maple Leafs' Terry Sawchuk
D. The Bruins' Gerry Cheevers

10.14 Which NHL team holds the record for most consecutive playoff appearances?
A. The Detroit Red Wings
B. The Chicago Blackhawks
C. The Boston Bruins
D. The Montreal Canadiens

10.15 How many Russians have their names engraved on the Stanley Cup?
A. One
B. Two
C. Three
D. Four

10.16 Since 1967 expansion, how many Stanley Cup finals were decided only in the seventh game?
A. Three finals
B. Four finals
C. Five finals
D. Six finals

10.17 Who was the youngest player to score a Stanley
Cup winner in NHL history?
A. The Bruins' Bobby Orr
B. The Oilers' Craig Simpson
C. The Maple Leafs' Ted Kennedy
D. The Canadiens' Henri Richard

THE MIRACLE ON 33RD STREET
(AND OTHER TRUE STORIES)
Answers

10.1 **B. Conference Finals—Game six against the
Devils.**
Perhaps the most prophetic fan signboard of the 1994
playoffs, simply, but cleverly, read "MESSiah," and after
guaranteeing "We'll win tonight" before game six to
stay alive in the Conference finals, and then locking it
with a natural hat trick, Messier proved again he could
lead the faithful to the promised land of the Cup finals
and hockey's silver chalice. It was won in a classic
seven-game final series by MESSiah's Stanley Cup winning goal, ending 54 years of Ranger exile.

10.2 **A. Paul Coffey.**
Few playoff teams have shattered more individual
league records than the dynasty era of the Edmonton
Oilers. As they freight-trained through four quick playoff rounds in 1985, losing just three games before claim-
ing their second Cup, Gretzky & Co. established an
array of almost unbeatable records, including Coffey's
one-year playoff record for most goals, assists and
points by a defenseman.

THE NHL'S TOP SCORING PLAYOFF DEFENSEMEN

	Player	Team	Season	GP	G	A	TP
1	P. Coffey	Oilers	1985	18	12	25	37
2	B. Leetch	Rangers	1994	23	11	23	34
3	A. MacInnis	Flames	1989	18	7	24	31
4	D. Potvin	Isles	1981	18	8	17	25
5	R. Bourque	Bruins	1991	19	7	18	25
6	B. Orr	Bruins	1972	15	5	19	24

Current to 1993-94

10.3   C. Johnny Bower.

The oldest goalie in NHL playoff history is Bower, who was 44 years, four months and 28 days old on April 6, 1969, his last post-season game. Patrick and Plante, both 44, were younger than Bower by a month and two months respectively. Hall was 39 years old in his last playoff match.

10.4   B. Wayne Connelly.

Connelly scored the NHL's first ever penalty shot in playoff action on April 9, 1968 against the Kings' Terry Sawchuk. It was awarded after Dale Rolfe interfered with the North Star forward on a clean break. Connelly made no mistake, skating straight in and roofing it over Sawchuk's stick side. Three previous penalty shots in playoff overtime—by Lionel Conacher in 1937, Alex Shibicky in 1937 and Virgil Johnson in 1944—all failed.

10.5   C. The Lincoln Tunnel.

The "Tunnel Series" was played between Madison Square Garden and Meadowlands Arena, a short six-mile drive from Manhattan to East Rutherford through the Lincoln Tunnel underneath the Hudson River.

10.6   B. Two times.
In NHL history, 15 teams have reached the Cup finals after finishing below .500 during the regular season, but only the 1938 Chicago Blackhawks (14–25–9) and the 1949 Maple Leafs (22–25–13) succeeded in winning the Stanley Cup despite their abysmal records. The 1938 'Hawks were longshots but upset favoured Toronto, a team 20 points better during the regular season. In 1949, top-seeded Detroit was blown out in the finals by the fourth-place Maple Leafs, who played way over their heads to become the first NHL team to claim three consecutive Stanley Cups. Both underdog teams, 1938 'Hawks and 1949 Leafs, swept the Cup finals in four straight.

10.7   A. San Jose's Vlastimil Kroupa.
One of 40 rookies in the 1994 playoffs, Kroupa, was the youngest NHLer to skate in post-season play at 19 years, 11 days old. The Czech Republic defenseman, drafted second round, 45th overall in 1993, scored 3 points and had a -3 in 14 playoff games.

10.8   B. Stephane Matteau.
When Mike Keenan acquired Matteau hours before the 1994 trading deadline, the ex-New York coach knew what his team needed over the stretch in the playoffs: a big, young aggressive forward with desire and attitude who wheels well in traffic and anticipates the play. For that reason, Keenan brought Matteau from Calgary when he was Chicago's GM and coach and, then, to New York to become one of the final pieces in the Rangers playoff puzzle. Matteau came through in the clutch, scoring sudden-death goals in two multiple-overtime games against the Devils, including game seven's thriller which put the Blueshirts into the Stanley Cup finals.

10.9   B. The Chicago Blackhawks.

Almost 50% of the 1938 champion Blackhawks were Americans. Eight U.S. players—Mike Karakas, Carl Voss, Alex Levinsky, Doc Romnes, Louis Trudel, Carl Dahlstrom, Roger Jenkins and Virgil Johnson—skated to Stanley Cup victory for Chicago, a hand-picked team managed and owned by Major Frederic McLaughlin, the Chicago hockey pioneer who named his club in honour of the Black Hawk division he commanded during World War One.

10.10   D. Ron Hextall.

The first three times that the Conn Smythe trophy was awarded to a player on the losing team, the Cup-winners were the Canadiens; first in 1966 Detroit's Roger Crozier won it, then in 1968 Chicago's Glenn Hall and next, in 1976, Philadelphia's Reggie Leach. Hextall, only the fourth NHLer ever to win playoff MVP on a losing side, is different because his 1987 Conn Smythe came against Edmonton (not Montreal).

10.11   D. It has never happened.

Goaltenders have a perfect record against shooters in penalty shots in the Cup final action, stopping seven of seven, the most recent by the Rangers' Mike Richter against Vancouver's Pavel Pure in game four of the 1994 finals.

10.12   B. Between $1,000 and $1,500.

Small in comparison to New York's 1994 Stanley Cup earnings ($1-million shared among team members— about $46,000 per player), the 1940 Cup winners each received $1,200 from the league, a considerable sum in 1940 when the average hockey salary was $3,500. Each Ranger got another $500 from the club.

10.13 A. The Canadiens' Gump Worsley.
The Gumper played maskless when the Canadiens won back-to-back Stanley Cups in 1968 and 1969 (as did opposing goalie Glenn Hall for St. Louis). The next year, when Boston won the championship, Cheevers was sporting his famous white mask with the black stitch marks. After that, all Cup-winning goalies, including Ken Dryden, Bernie Parent and Billy Smith, wore face protection. Worsley, one of the last "old guard" goaltenders, played 21 seasons and waited until near-retirement, 1973–74, before reluctantly putting on his first mask.

10.14 C. The Boston Bruins.
Harry Sinden's Bruins have made the playoffs 27 times from 1968 through 1994, the longest consecutive post-season streak in NHL history. During that run they have won two Stanley Cups (1970 & 1972), made the finals five times, the second and third rounds ten times, and not beyond the first round ten times. Their greatest playoff foe is the Canadiens, who have defeated Boston in 12 playoff series, twice in the Cup finals.

10.15 D. Four.
The first four Russian-trained players to have their names on the Stanley Cup are all 1994 New York Rangers. Alexei Kovalev (21 points) and Sergei Zubov (19 points) were the third- and fourth-highest scoring Rangers in the 1994 playoffs (after Brian Leetch and Mark Messier). Teammates Sergei Nemchinov (7 points) and Alexander Karpovtsev (4 points) are the other Russian Cup winners.

10.16 A. Three finals.
In 27 NHL post-seasons (1967 to 1994), only three seventh and deciding games have been necessary: 1971's Blackhawks/Canadiens nail-biter at Chicago Stadium

(Montreal 3 - Chicago 2), 1987's Oilers/Flyers final at Northlands Coliseum (Edmonton 3 - Philadelphia 1) and 1994's Rangers/Canucks cliffhanger at Madison Square Garden (New York 3 - Vancouver 2). Since 1939, when the NHL expanded the finals to a best-of-seven format, a seventh game has happened only ten times.

10.17 C. The Maple Leafs' Ted Kennedy.

Kennedy, the youngest NHLer to score a Cup-winning goal, was 21 years, 4 months old when he fired a long shot past Canadiens' Bill Durnan that potted the 1947 Stanley Cup for Toronto, a team stocked with the youngest Cup winners in NHL history.

SOLUTIONS TO GAMES

GAME 1: PASSING THE PUCK FANTASTIC

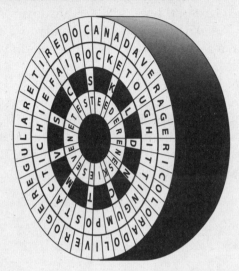

GAME 2: TRASH TALK

Part 1

1. John Ziegler
2. Jack Kent Cooke
3. Foster Hewitt

4. Cam Neely
5. Harold Ballard
6. Michael Eisner

7. Bobby Hull

Part 2

1. Gordie Howe
2. Glenn Hall
3. Frank Arthur Griffiths, Sr.
7. Alan Eagleson

4. Chris Pronger
5. Al Iafrate
6. Harry Neale
8. Reporter Steve Simmons

GAME 3: THE TOP EXPANSION PICKS

1. F
2. D
3. O
4. G
5. M
6. J
7. K
8. E

9. L
10. C
11. A
12. H
13. N
14. B
15. I

GAME 4: THE CROSSNUMBER

GAME 5: THE NHL CAPTAINS

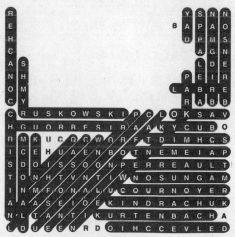

Emile BOUCHARD, nine-year Canadien captain from 1948 to 1956, never won any scoring races, nor did he take home any individual NHL awards, but his leadership was the foundation upon which scoring greats like Maurice Richard, Jean Beliveau and Dickie Moore could excel. There were better defensemen on Montreal's blueline, like Doug Harvey, but Bouchard kept the team together, winning two Stanley Cups during his captaincy.

GAME 6: NUMBER CRUNCHING

1. 39	7. 1971
2. 17	8. 215
3. 47	9. 23
4. 6	10. 1988
5. 802	11. 52
6. 2421	12. 92

GAME 7: THE CROSSWORD

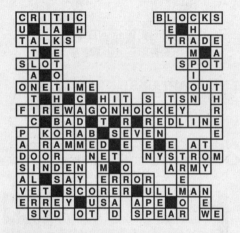

GAME 8: THE 500-GOAL CLUB

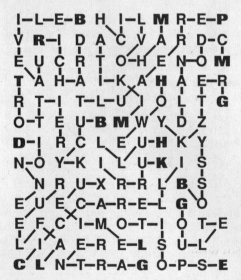

GAME 9: "FOR TEE-OFF TIME INFO, CALL 1-800-U-BLEW-IT"

1. Toronto's Maple Leaf Gardens. With San Jose in town to play the Leafs in the Conference semis, Toronto fans bait their predacious opponents with a little play on words. No easy victims, the Cinderella Sharks only got hooked in game seven. The runner-up sign slogan at the Gardens: "The Only Thing The Sharks Will Bite Is Dust."

2. Dallas' Reunion Arena. No strangers to the playoff experience, especially after two Super Bowl victories by their Cowboys, Dallas fans serve notice they want to add the Stanley Cup to their collection of championships.

3. Montreal Forum. Montreal fans champion the 1993 Cup-winning Canadiens one last time before they get unceremoniously eliminated from 1994's first playoff round by Boston, 4-3.

4. Vancouver's Pacific Coliseum. Broadcaster and popular Canadian redneck Don Cherry is welcomed by Canuck fans, who mix apples and oranges, er . . . cherries, at the playoff finals against the Big Apple's Rangers.

5. Chicago Stadium. Before a Blackhawk home game, a recorded version of Wayne Messmer singing "The Star-Spangled Banner" is played to honour Messmer, the acclaimed Chicago anthem singer, who is in hospital after suffering serious injuries from gunfire, the victim of a parking lot robbery attempt.

6. Nassau Veterans' Memorial Coliseum. Diehard Islander fans keep the faith after being bludgeoned 17-1 in three games in the Conference quarterfinals against the Rangers.

7. Detroit's Joe Louis Arena. Four nights after scoring his 500th NHL goal in Los Angeles, 14-year NHL veteran Dino Ciccarelli comes home to a hero's welcome.

8. Ottawa Civic Centre. In the midst of a month-long, 20- game slump, Senator fans seek rejuvenation from fan- favourite and retired Ottawa journeyman Brad Marsh, the living embodiment of perseverance in the face of adversity.

9. The Pond of Anaheim. Novice hockey fans of the Mighty Ducks get their feet wet at the Pond.

10. Washington's U.S. Air Arena. After serving a 21-game suspension, Capital tough guy Dale Hunter finally plays his first home game of 1993-94.

11. San Jose Arena. In game seven of the Conference quarterfinals, the third-year Sharks gorge themselves on the Red Wings, whose fans still throw octopus on the ice at playoff time. This Detroit tradition dates back to the 1950s when the Wings won Cups by sweeping the two best-of-seven playoff rounds eight games (or tentacles) straight.

12. Buffalo's Memorial Auditorium. Sabre fans love their Russian superstar Alexander Mogilny, comparing him to one of history's greatest generals from ancient times.

13. Hartford Civic Center. With the last-place Senators in town, Whaler fans seize the moment and gloat over their own team's slightly less dire position in the standings.

14. New Jersey's Meadowlands Arena. After a thrilling seven-game series over Buffalo, the Devils play game one of the 1994 Conference quarterfinals at home to a half-empty house. One New York newspaper wonders why and asks New Jersey season ticket holders to mail in their explanations of what they were doing instead. The next game, one Devil fan skates around the issue, trying to "write" the wrong on a signboard.

ACKNOWLEDGEMENTS

The following publishers and organizations have given permission for use of quoted material:

From *The Hockey News*, various excerpts. Reprinted by permission of *The Hockey News*, a division of GTC Transcontinental Publishing Inc.

From "Big League," written by Tom Cochrane. Reprinted by permission of Tom Cochrane and Gold Mountain.

From *Gordie: A Hockey Legend*, by Roy MacSkimming. Copyright © 1994. Published by Greystone Books, a division of Douglas & McIntyre Ltd. Reprinted by permission of Douglas & McIntyre Ltd.

Care has been taken to trace ownership of copyright material contained in this book. The publishers welcome any information that will enable them to rectify any reference or credit in subsequent editions.

The author gratefully acknowledges the help of Russ Conway, Phil Pritchard at the Hockey Hall of Fame, Steve Dryden at *The Hockey News*, Brian Lewis and Greg Inglis at the National Hockey League, Ted Baker at the Ontario Hockey League, CFCF-TV in Montreal, Gerry Helper, Pat Park, Igor Kuperman, Bill Tuele, Barry Watkins, Greg Bouris, Jim DeMaria, Laurent Benoit and Russ Ramsay, as well as factchecker Allen Bishop, graphic artist Ivor Tiltin and puzzle designer Adrian van Vlaardingen.

HOCKEY TRIVIA'S READER REBOUND

Do you have a favourite hockey trivia question that stumps everyone? Or one that needs an answer? Write us, and if we haven't used it before, we may include it in next year's trivia book. We can only pick about 25 questions and answers, so give us your best shot.

We'll make sure every question selected is credited with the sender's name and area of residence. Just two rules: 1) Duplications will be decided by earliest postmark; and 2) Sorry, we can't answer letters individually.

Write us at

HOCKEY TRIVIA
c/o DON WEEKES
P.O. BOX 221
MONTREAL, QUEBEC
CANADA
H4A 3P5

Please print

NAME:_____AGE:_____

PLACE OF
RESIDENCE:_____

FAVOURITE
TEAM:_____
FAVOURITE
PLAYER(S):_____

YOUR
QUESTION:_____
_____
_____
_____

ANSWER:_____
_____
_____
_____
_____
_____

(continued on next page)

Even if you don't have a trivia question, we'd like to hear from you.

READER SURVEY

In future books on hockey trivia, would you like questions that are:

Easier ___   About The Same ___   Harder ___

Would you like more games ___ ; or fewer games ___

What kinds of questions or games do you like the most, or would like more of? (i.e., multiple choice, true or false, fill-in-the-blanks, cross-words, etc.)

_____

_____

_____

_____

OTHER
*COMMENTS:*_____

_____

_____

_____

_____

_____

THE OPINION CORNER
What do you like most about hockey?_____

_____

_____

How would you like the game to change? (i.e., shootouts, two referees, etc.) _____

_____

_____

When and how did you first get interested in hockey?

_____

_____

_____